To

From

Date

THE KINGDOM OF GOD
AND ITS RIGHTEOUSNESS

THE KINGDOM OF GOD
AND ITS RIGHTEOUSNESS

APOSTLE G. MALDONADO

Our Mission:

Called to bring the supernatural power of God to this generation

The Kingdom of God and Its Righteousness

First Edition 2008

ISBN-13: 978-1-59272-266-2

Cover Design by: ERJ Publicaciones

ERJ Publicaciones

13651 SW 143 Ct., Suite 101, Miami, FL 33186

Tel: (305) 382-3171 - Fax: (305) 675-5770

Category: Kingdom

Printed in USA

This book is dedicated to the one person who has been my most faithful friend and everlasting counselor, the precious Holy Spirit. He is the One who fills me with the revelation and wisdom of the Father and the One whose guidance has led me to have a deeper understanding of the Kingdom of God and its righteousness, as it is established on Earth.

My most sincere thanks to a man who, because of his great generosity and heart for the Kingdom, has shared with me the precious revelations given to him by the Holy Spirit during the many years he has served in the ministry.

Apostle Alan Vincent, I take this opportunity to publicly express my appreciation for the time you have invested in me. You have been like a father to me and a role model in the area of apostolic revelation. Thanks to your teachings, my eyes were opened, allowing the Holy Spirit to reveal to me new dimensions of the Kingdom of God and its righteousness. Without your invaluable support, this book would never have been written. Thank you!

TABLE OF CONTENT

INTRODUCTION

Can you hear their cry? Can you feel their pain? Can you see the faces of thousands of children, teenagers, men, and women? Are you able to hear the cry of nature coming from the sea, land, valleys, mountains, rivers, and deserts? Creation is crying out for redemption; it needs to be redeemed from its curse. Redemption! Salvation! Justice! Peace! Love! The Son of God heard the cry and paved the way. He came to Earth and brought His Kingdom with Him—the unshakeable Kingdom! Jesus came to proclaim the Kingdom of God and its righteousness: justice for the poor in spirit, the broken-hearted, the impoverished, the sick, and everyone who cries out for justice.

Anyone who is close to God can experience the pain He feels for mankind. The need for redemption is great in the heart of the Creator. He cries out in great pain and anguish for the salvation of His children; for this reason, He sent Jesus—the Prince of Peace—to restore His Kingdom among men.

Since the day I met the Lord, He has brought me closer and closer to His heart. I feel so close to Him that His pain has become my pain. From the beginning, I have been passionate about rescuing the lost: those who have yet to meet God, discover their purpose, destiny, and their relationship with the Heavenly Father. I am passionately committed to bringing hope to the people who live in spiritual, emotional, and financial darkness; more so, knowing that our Father has an abundance of treasures in His home waiting for anyone who dares take them by force. My passion has always consisted in sharing the good news of the Kingdom; to remove the spiritual veil from their eyes so they can see how far they have strayed from home. The Father waits for His children with open arms. He waits for them to return home so He can place the ring on their finger, dress them in fine linen, and prepare a welcome feast to rejoice for their return: *"...for this my son was dead and is alive again; he was lost and is found..."*

The Kingdom of God—the Father's House—is the divine government in which mankind can live in complete freedom, justice, and abundance of material wealth. We live in a time where the restoration of all things is taking place. One main area that is being restored is the establishment of the Kingdom of God on Earth. For many years, the church has believed in Jesus and preached the message of salvation. Unfortunately, it has failed to include the Father's House and its numerous privileges available for us to enjoy while still on Earth because they still believe one must wait for heaven to enter it. However, the Holy Spirit—the One who guides us to the truth and reveals the Father—tells us we must establish the Kingdom on Earth and live according to its laws and benefits, *today*. We do not have to wait for heaven in order to enjoy the benefits of healing, to be free from bondage, to attain justice, to stop the curse of poverty in our lives, or to defeat Satan. Jesus defeated the enemy at the cross by taking upon Himself our sin, pain, and sickness, and by returning to us the authority and power to bind the powers of darkness on Earth and loosen the blessings stored in heaven for us.

I invite you to enter into the most fascinating revelation that is flooding our church today: the revelation of the Kingdom of God and its righteousness. In my diligent search of discovering the heart of the Father, He has revealed to me some of the precious pearls of His immense wisdom which I want to share with you. We live in times in which a reformation, transformation, and restoration are taking place. The war against the kingdom of darkness becomes more violent as time goes by because the Kingdom of God is being established to the ends of the Earth. The heavenly city is establishing itself over our cities and nations, bringing the righteousness of the Kingdom by the power of the Holy Spirit; bringing light to darkness; order to confusion; justice to oppression; and love to the heart of men. Why? Because the Word declares: "*...let the whole Earth be filled with His glory...*" "*...glory as of the only begotten of the Father.*" "*He is called the God of the whole Earth.*" "*...and the government will be upon His shoulder...*" "*Of the increase of His government there will be no end...*"

"...to order it and establish it with judgment and justice..." "From that time forward, even forever..."

"The time is fulfilled, and the Kingdom of God is at hand..."

Chapter 1

THE RESTORATION
OF THE KINGDOM

In the beginning, God created the heavens and the Earth, and when He looked upon His creation, He declared it was "all" good. God created all things, and as the crown of His creation, He created man in His likeness and image. He gave man lordship by delegating His authority to Adam so he could govern the Earth, together with his Creator. Man joined the relationship between God the Father, God the Son, and God the Holy Spirit. He was created to dwell with God and to share and govern together with Him.

"26Then God said, "Let Us make man in Our image, according to Our likeness; let them have dominion over the fish of the sea, over the birds of the air, and over the cattle, over all the Earth and over every creeping thing that creeps on the Earth." Genesis 1.26

From the moment of creation, God established the following principle: Only a human being—a spirit with a soul who dwells in a physical body—can exercise power and authority on Earth. Consequently, after breathing His breath of life upon man, God delegated His authority over him to govern and exercise lordship over His creation.

"7And the LORD God formed man of the dust of the ground, and breathed into his nostrils the breath of life; and man became a living being." Genesis 2.7

When Adam was connected to the spiritual realm, through God's breath of life, he received the authority to exercise lordship over the Earth—a body without the divine breath of life cannot govern. The authority Adam received was delegated which meant he could only exercise it as long as he was in submission and connected to the Kingdom or government of God.

God Gives Adam Specific Instructions on How to Govern the Garden of Eden

"¹⁶And the LORD God commanded the man, saying, "Of every tree of the garden you may freely eat; ¹⁷but of the tree of the knowledge of good and evil you shall not eat, for in the day that you eat of it you shall surely die." Genesis 2.16, 17

Up to that point in time, man was without sin, and his relationship with the Father was free and unrestricted; that was the period of innocence, when man dwelled within the Kingdom of God where sickness, pain, or suffering were unheard of because he lived a life solely dependent on God. Adam breathed the life of his Creator. Therefore, he had no need to be independent from Him. As long as he lived in total submission and obedience to the Father, he was under the constant protection and government of God's Kingdom. There, Adam was immune to Satan's attacks—God's enemy. In the beginning, man was immortal and lived in a Kingdom that was absolutely impenetrable and which Satan could not invade. From what we know, it is easy to conclude that the impenetrability of the Kingdom was due to the obedience or dependence of the will of man to the will or government of God.

What caused man to fall into temptation? Man was tempted in the area of his independence. The enemy tempted Adam with the idea of gaining the ability to govern himself and become like God. Consequently, Adam took the corresponding action to his independence without realizing that this action was equivalent to rebellion. However, mankind was not created to govern itself; it does not possess that ability. The only thing it has is the freedom to *choose* who to be governed by: God or Satan. Because of this, if we are deceived by the lie of independence, Satan will automatically take control over our lives and everything that belongs to us.

What is the definition of the word *independence*? The word *independence* is defined as: not subject to; not relying on (God), or to live totally separated from (God). In other words, it is the autonomy of human will. This separation or independence is equal to rebellion. In simpler terms, the New Testament refers to this as: *acting according to the flesh; to be selfish, self-sufficient, and to seek to satisfy the desires of the flesh and not of the spirit, which is connected to God.* This is why the Bible teaches that we should crucify the flesh, everyday, and deny its rights in order to live according to the spirit.

We can sum this up by saying that independence means to live outside the direct government of God; to make decisions without depending on Him or taking into account His perfect will or council.

How did this temptation take place?

"⁴Then the serpent said to the woman, "You will not surely die. ⁵For God knows that in the day you eat of it your eyes will be opened, and you will be like God, knowing good and evil." ⁶So when the woman saw that the tree was good for food, that it was pleasant to the eyes, and a tree desirable to make one wise, she took of its fruit and ate. She also gave to her husband with her, and he ate. ⁷Then the eyes of both of them were opened, and they knew that they were naked; and they sewed fig leaves together and made themselves coverings." Genesis 3.4-7

The enemy's suggestion to mankind has always been: "Why live under the government and authority of God, why submit to Him, if within you resides the power needed to grow and become God's equal? You are strong enough to do it in your own strength! Why not dare to do it yourself? Your life will not change except for the fact that you will have the same power and authority of God. You will not be required to be subjected to His government, but rather, you will be in charge of your own life!" This is the most destructive lie man has chosen to believe; it is the foundation of all religions and sects from around the world which encourage men to live their own lives as they see fit—*independent* and *self-governing*. Most religions teach that man does not need God. Adam and Eve were unable to resist the temptation of becoming independent. Before they realized what had taken place when they made their decision, they found themselves outside the protection of the Kingdom. That was exactly what Satan wanted.

He knew that if he could take the spirit of independence and thrust it into the heart of man, he would successfully separate him from the Father. As a matter of fact, this was that same spirit that caused Satan to fall. It is also the strategy he used, and still uses, to influence mankind to walk away from the Kingdom.

Adam was surprised when he was forced to leave the Kingdom, after he chose to govern himself. The moment he stepped outside God's government—Kingdom—he became vulnerable and unsheltered, and his fall came quickly. His choice to become independent pierced a gap in the impenetrable Kingdom. The words spoken by the serpent encouraged man to acquire the knowledge of good and evil and to become equal to God—an action that seemed harmless and provokingly attractive. However, when the serpent presented Adam with the tempting offer to discover the truth about good and evil, he cunningly chose not to reveal the fact that their decision would lead to death and complete separation from their source of life. In the end, when the decision to disobey was carried out by Adam and Eve, they realized—too late—what had taken place. In a blinking of an eye, in a badly made decision, they were removed from the government of God and placed under the oppression of Satan's government.

It was never Adam and Eve's intention to sin. They did not *plan* on sinning. They did, however, allow their curiosity to get the best of them; causing them to give into the tempting desire of tasting the visually appetizing fruit that would allow them to "become equal to God." Unfortunately, their decision led to their downfall and to their expulsion from the presence of their Creator. They were disconnected from their source of life and identity; thus, procuring the foothold for Satan to legally govern over them and the only way God would lose His influence over their lives.

Good intentions are not enough to do what is right
before the Father. We need more than that
to remain under His protection
and receive His blessings.

What happened after man sinned?

When the man and woman accepted the suggestion from God's enemy, the Father's protection was removed from their lives along with the delegated authority to govern the Earth; this was precisely Satan's goal from the beginning because he wanted to have total dominion for himself and the authority to govern the Earth. As a result, God removed his presence and man was cut off from the source of life and the communion, that up to that point, he had enjoyed with the Father. It was sad and painful when Adam and Eve became *independent* from their Creator.

Adam's step into independence was the first towards the destruction of mankind. Unfortunately, it continues to take place today. The sin of independence and the curse that came over their lives have been passed down from generation to generation. We know this to be true when we read about the countless lives that end because of accidents, sickness, or tragedies caused by their decision to live independently from God—independence causes God's protection to be removed from our lives.

The desire for independence is one of the most powerful temptations that today's leaders and individuals have to deal with; especially if they are gifted, talented, and wealthy because such things gives them a false sense of not needing God. The lives of people who give into this temptation are destroyed. Therefore, no man or woman has the luxury to live independently from God.

Satan's need or want for independence caused him to fall and be thrown out of heaven. Adam and Eve, far from having the intention to sin, only hoped to continue living morally correct while using their own moral or righteous strength to become one with God again; at least, that's what they assumed would happen. However, what they were led to believe would take place never did. As a matter of fact, after their fall, all of creation fell under Satan's lordship. That is, not only had man walked into a life of damnation, but also *all* of creation. Everything that was originally under the authority and government of man went to be under the authority and government of Satan; this is why entire nations, families, and individuals suffer the curse of sickness, pain, and death—nature also suffers disorders in its performance. Many people ask, "If God claims to be a good and righteous God, why are there so many people in the world dying of hunger? Why are destruction, sickness, earthquakes, hurricanes, and abused/mistreated children every day events in today's world?" The answer to these questions is simple: Man is governing himself; he is independent and living outside of God's Kingdom. In other words, it is not God's fault but of those who choose to live without Him.

What can we learn from this?

The moral lesson is clear and fundamental: No one can live independent of his Creator because that only leads to destruction. Adam learned the lesson too late; that independence is painful and leads only to death. *Independence is the root that bears the fruit of sin.* Therefore, when we live independently from God, we have no strength to resist the devil or his demons. No one has the sufficient spiritual strength to resist the devil on his own because the first man—Adam—surrendered that authority. Even Satan, being one that was created by God, was under the authority and government of mankind. Unfortunately, man failed to exercise his authority; instead, he chose to accept the devil's lies. Satan was less than man, but man made him greater when he surrendered his authority and territory. Consequently, man does not have the inner strength to resist the temptation to sin. The only way for mankind to overcome temptation and the enemy is to be joined with God.

> Independence is the root
> that bears the fruit of sin.

Today, millions of people are unable to resist temptation because they govern themselves and live in total rebellion to divine laws. Many want to stop their addiction to pornography, their compulsive desire to eat, to consume drugs, to live, practice adultery, take sleeping pills, stop deceiving people, and more, but they do not have the inner strength to be free because they choose not to submit to God.

From one moment to the next, the sin of man and Satan's newly acquired authority, turned the world up-side-down; everything was in chaos. And yet, while this was taking place, our Heavenly Father did not stand idly merely watching as His creation was being destroyed. No! He immediately took action and provided the means through which man could regain his position and authority in the Kingdom.

How did God restore the Kingdom back to man? When Adam's downfall took place, God had two options: The first was to judge the devil, destroy his kingdom, and cast him into hell until the day of the final judgment; the second was to find a way to pay the wages of man's sin—to pay the price required for man to reenter the Kingdom—and later destroy Satan.

The first option was not viable because if God, by His righteousness, judged Satan and his kingdom, He would also have to judge man by that same measure—being that man was now part of the enemy's territory—resulting in *all* of humanity to end up in hell.

The second option was to find a man without sin, able to pay the price on behalf of everyone and restore the authority on Earth; thus, through that sacrifice, saving mankind from suffering the same damnation Satan will undoubtedly suffer. For God so loved the world that He decided to save it by sending His one and only Son as payment for the restitution, reconciliation (with Him), and restoration of the Kingdom on Earth.

Many people ask, "If God is more powerful than Satan, why has He not destroyed him?" God cannot destroy the devil because His righteousness would obligate Him to also destroy man. Because of His righteousness, God keeps the door of salvation open for every human being, and in the process, He has to allow the devil's lies, deceitfulness, and government to operate (for a short period of time); this is why He has not judged or destroyed him—yet!

The devil continues to deceive people by convincing them of the lie, conveying to those who fall for it that they have the right to be independent because, *supposedly*, being independent is preferable to the "oppressive, benevolent, and totalitarian" government of God. Some people opt to live in bondage to sin rather than submit to the government of God. With pride they declare their "independence, intelligence, and freedom" while the chains of slavery that binds them can be heard rattling wherever they go. They are not happy! They have no inner life! They do not realize the extent to which the enemy has them in bondage. In reality, they are far from being free; they live in constant oppression, torment, and in total darkness because their vision of the truth has been distorted.

Living independently from God has led man to live in depression, sickness, suffering, pain, loneliness, poverty, ruin, and sin. Therefore, our Heavenly Father needed a man (a human being) who did not conform to this world; one who was obedient to His Word, who obeyed His will, and who would restore the Kingdom. Why did God need a *man* to do such things? Why not use *His* power and supremacy?

"[31]And behold, you will conceive in your womb and bring forth a Son, and shall call His name JESUS." Luke 1.31

God had to restrict Himself to the same principles He had initially established from the beginning of creation: Every spirit that wants to do something on Earth must have a physical body. It was that principle that led God to search for a man capable of successfully saving mankind. Consequently, He had to become a man, so through His death, Adam's descendants—mankind—would be saved. His resurrection would enable Him to redeem the Earth from Satan's control and totally destroy the kingdom of darkness and its works. Jesus came to Earth, was born of a virgin, and lived thirty three and a half years in total obedience to the Father. He died—shed His blood on the cross— and took upon Himself every sin committed by humanity. He descended to hell where He spent three days and nights for our iniquity, and on the third day, He was raised from the dead having conquered the authority to govern the Earth.

From the moment of His birth to the moment He ascended into heaven, Jesus lived in absolute dependence to the Father. As a man, He had supreme obedience toward God in every area of His human life. He allowed Himself to be guided by the Holy Spirit during His ministry. Because of this, He was able to establish the Kingdom of God on Earth.

"30I can of Myself do nothing. As I hear, I judge; and My judgment is righteous, because I do not seek My own will but the will of the Father who sent Me." John 5.30

The authority in which Jesus operated to heal the sick, teach, preach, and cast out demons came from His total obedience to the Father. He was the same as an average man but in complete dependence to God. The difference between the first Adam and the second—Jesus—was that the first decided to live independently from God, while the second chose to live totally dependent on the Father. When Jesus was raised, as a Man and an obedient Son, He was given all power and authority in heaven and on Earth. With His resurrection, He birthed a new type of man—one full of glory, victorious, and reconnected to the source of His Creator.

"18And Jesus came and spoke to them, saying, "All authority has been given to Me in heaven and on Earth." Matthew 28.18

The government of God
operates only in those who obey His will,
and the enemy cannot touch them.

What did Jesus do when He recovered the authority? Jesus did everything the Father asked Him to do in order to recover the lost authority, and later, He gave it to the church—the average believer.

Now, the Kingdom of Heaven is established on Earth by the children of God.

"³²Do not fear, little flock, for it is your Father's good pleasure to give you the Kingdom." Luke 12.32

Let us remember that the Kingdom of God only operates in individuals who obey and carry out His will, completely and without question. Within those parameters, the enemy cannot touch us. When we act in total dependence of the Holy Spirit, we become immune to the enemy's attacks. However, if we choose to live independently from God, we open a gap in the Kingdom, the enemy steals away our authority, and we are led to total destruction.

Jesus Transferred His Kingdom into Our Hands

"¹³He has delivered us from the power of darkness and conveyed us into the Kingdom of the Son of His love..." Colossians 1.13

The temptation of living independently or to live in rebellion continues to be active even after Jesus was raised from the dead. He did not redeem us from that temptation because that is one area we must learn to deal with; the ability to choose which path to take is part of our freedom of choice. We can choose to live dependent on God or independent from Him as an act of our will.

The conflict between these two kingdoms—light and darkness—is always present. Man has the freedom to choose which kingdom he will depend on and who governs over him.

Jesus opened the door of salvation and reconciliation with the Heavenly Father. He paved the way, paying for it with His blood so we can be free from the bondage of slavery and able to *decide* if we want to be free or continue in bondage to Satan. The freedom the devil offers is false, misleading, and deceiving because he uses that freedom to bind us to the passions of our flesh. God suggests we choose life and blessings but many still choose death, instead.

What is the first message Jesus preached on Earth?

"²...and saying, "Repent, for the Kingdom of Heaven is at hand!"
Matthew 3.2

Jesus did not come to preach on forgiveness of sins but on the Kingdom of God, with repentance as a condition to enter the Kingdom; hence, the first word Jesus pronounced was *repent*.

What is the meaning of the word *repent*?

The word **repent** is the Greek word *metonoeo*, and it means: to change one's mind and lifestyle. Jesus said that if we fail to live with the right attitude of dependence, it will be impossible for God to deal with our sins. It seems impossible to change the way we live, if first, we do not change the way we think. Genuine repentance causes a permanent change in our mentality, turning it into a Kingdom mentality—one that is totally renewed.

According to Jesus, what should we repent for?

We need to repent for the choice to govern ourselves—the independence that marked our previous status of damnation. Afterwards, we must live in line to the government of God and learn to depend solely on Him—totally abandoning our past way of life. Jesus not only teaches that we need to repent for our choice to control our own lives but also to return to the Kingdom of God, being that it is a Kingdom with total authority and order over those who enter it.

Illustration: Every religion in the world operates under the same pattern. They teach good moral principles but fail to depend on God to carry them out. They influence their people to live in their own strength while generating a set of useless rituals. They do this because no one has the power to be good on their own. This is the sin of independence; the first one we should repent from. No one can save themselves nor achieve true success with their own capabilities or wisdom; it is only when we surrender our lives to God for Him to govern over us that we will experience a genuine change and true success.

It is easy to *say* "the Kingdom of God has come to us," although, to *know* if this is true, we should consider the following questions: Who is in charge of your life, God or you? Who makes the decisions, God or you? To whom and to what do you dedicate most of your time? Why are you in school trying to obtain that degree? Who decided which career you should follow? Why do you live where you are? Did God choose your home or did you? Who led you to buy or establish that business? Who decided who your partner should be? How do you invest your money? Who led you to the church you attend? Who led you to marry your spouse? Who leads you to take the decisions you make?

Decisions based on the will of God lead
to success in the world and the Kingdom.

You have two alternatives: to be governed by God or to govern yourself in your own strength. If you choose the latter, you will allow the spirit of independence to enter your heart. Consequently, you will be outside the Kingdom and the will of God, governed by Satan, and subject to the kingdom of darkness. In this war, there are no vacancies; either you are in one kingdom or the other. Independence gives way to the sin of rebellion against the Kingdom of God. On the other hand, if independence is cut off, sin stops and rebellion dissipates.

Illustration: The owner of a car finds a professional chauffer and tells him, "I have no idea how to drive this car. I have tried to learn all my life, but I always do the wrong thing and end up on the curb. Please, take total control. I will be very happy if, from this moment forward, I can be just a passenger."

The former illustration exemplifies the attitude of one who has truly repented and has no problem turning over total control of his life to the expert driver—God!

How do we know we are living in total obedience to the Kingdom and the will of its King?

Below are several characteristics that prove we are living dependent and obedient to the Kingdom and God:

❖ We recognize that Jesus is also God and absolute Lord of our lives and material wealth.

❖ We obey the voice of the Holy Spirit without complaining or questioning what He is asking us to do.

❖ We commit ourselves to obey His will before we know what He is going to ask.

❖ Our commitment to serve regardless of the circumstances, time, or place.

❖ Pleasing God exceeds our desire to please others or ourselves.

❖ We consider God as the source that supplies all our needs and wants.

❖ Knowing God and having a personal relationship with the Holy Spirit is an obsession in our lives.

❖ Our priority is Jesus above anyone else, including family.

❖ We choose to obey Jesus even when His request does not seem reasonable, comfortable, beneficial, or convenient.

❖ We decide to follow Jesus as disciples by taking our cross each day and denying the desires of our flesh.

This is what it means to live in total obedience and submission to the Kingdom and the will of its King. When we choose to live this way, we can earnestly say we are being governed by God and that His

Kingdom has entered our lives—of course, keeping in mind we are neither perfect nor flawless.

Millions of believers today are trying to change the world and establish the Kingdom of God in their families, cities, and churches. Unfortunately, unknowing to them, the Kingdom of God has not even entered their hearts or lives. Christians must understand that we cannot change a corrupt society and its moral values until we submit to God's government and authority. Everything we do: sacrifices, worship, and works are pointless if we disobey the laws of the Kingdom or the government of God.

Are there areas of disobedience in our lives? Could there be a trace of rebellion in our hearts towards the Kingdom and lordship of Jesus? Today, we must choose to make a commitment; to live dependent upon God, obeying Him by faith and by respecting the principles and commandments of His Kingdom. This is the only way we will see the glory of Jesus manifest in our homes and society.

Disobedience and rebellion
open doors for Satan's Kingdom
to enter our lives, home, and society.

Chapter 2

WHAT IS THE KINGDOM OF GOD?

Before we go into the subject of the Kingdom, we must ask the Holy Spirit to give us the wisdom and revelation to understand His mysteries. We must humble ourselves and recognize our hunger to know, understand, and obey the norms established by the Kingdom of God because the revelation cannot manifest without the desire to take action.

Few people today know the true meaning of God's Kingdom because it is not a customary subject taught in churches or Biblical institutes. Studies on the Kingdom are not part of the curriculum in the great theological institutions. Some people believe the Kingdom of God consists in attending church; others believe it can only be experienced in heaven, after Jesus returns for His church; some do not give it a second thought or may be unaware of its existence or the power it possesses. These are the reasons why so many who have been faithful church attendees for years have yet to experience change. It is extremely important to grasp the significant difference there is between attending church and entering the Kingdom of God.

The revelation of the Kingdom of God
has the power to change lives.

To better understand the Kingdom, we need a *Kingdom-mentality* because the Kingdom is a network of thoughts, lifestyle, principles, laws, and fundamentals that can only be understood thanks to the revelation the Holy Spirit supplies to a mind that is willing to accept it. The Kingdom challenges us to change our lives, completely. Right now, very few Christian leaders teach or preach on the Kingdom of God. They do, however, spend much time talking about denominations, religion, and other matters of lesser importance.

During His stay on Earth, Jesus mentioned the Kingdom and its righteousness over one hundred times and only twice did He mention the church. In general, if something is mentioned over one hundred times, it must be something very important. Now think: the most powerful man to have ever existed, the only One who was one hundred percent man and one hundred percent God, took the time to make the subject of the Kingdom of God and its righteousness the central theme of all His teachings. The subject was so important to Him that He included it in the Lord's Prayer establishing the importance of seeking it as a priority in our lives.

"²So He said to them, "When you pray, say: Our Father in heaven, hallowed be Your name. Your Kingdom come. Your will be done on Earth as it is in heaven." Luke 11.2

Many people, Christians, sects, theologians, authors, scientists, intellectuals, preachers, teachers, apostles, prophets, and pastors speak on the Kingdom of God, but in truth, they have no idea what it really is. They have not received the clear revelation of its true meaning or the impact it could have on every man's life.

Before diving into the subject matter of this chapter, let us look at the types of Kingdoms that have always existed throughout history and are still operating today. When we do, we will better understand the Kingdom or government of God. According to the book of Daniel, these are the governments that have existed:

❖ The Babylonian Empire. This empire was governed by one person—a tyrant. In theory, this government's system was perfect; however, for it to properly operate it needed a perfect head—you and I both know there is no perfect person who can fit this description; thus, this government failed and ceased to exist.

❖ The Persian Empire. This government was founded on law, in such a way, that once a law was approved it could not be invalidated or voided. However, any system and its man-created laws are imperfect. Therefore, sooner or later, it will produce injustice.

❖ The Greek Empire. This empire was governed by the power of intellect and founded on debate and argumentation (rhetoric) where the whole world had an opportunity to give their opinion. Accordingly, the will of the majority established the government. Today, we call this democracy.

I personally believe this is the most decent and reasonable of all known systems, although the opinion of the majority is rarely the right one; this is where we get the term "tyranny of the majority." The problem with this type of government is that it is based on modern humanism and synthetic thought where neither absolute truth nor clear and true leadership exist. Today, for example, most heads of democratic world government lead their people in accordance with the public opinion, economic convenience, influential groups, and the media.

❖ The Roman Empire. Like the Greek, the Roman Empire was a "people's government"; a democratic government represented by the Senate. This government was based on colonial ruling; controlling its people by arguing racial and political supremacy. It believed that it governed the people of other ethnic backgrounds for their own good. To successfully accomplish this, the empire used effective administration and its military force. This type of government, at its best, becomes a male dominant government that never allows its people to grow and mature in order to assume governmental responsibility.

❖ The Unshakeable Kingdom of God. This is a perfect government; sovereign, eternal, with absolute authority, and with an absolute King as its head. It is a totalitarian and benevolent government where everyone who chooses to submit to it finds complete and total freedom.

Man-made governments are imperfect;
but the Kingdom of God is perfect,
effective, and unshakeable.

It was important for us to understand the different types of governments or kingdoms that existed throughout history and recognize their imperfections. The Kingdom of God is the only one that merits the description of perfect, unshakeable, and effective. With this in mind, let us continue digging into this compelling subject.

We have seven kingdoms in operation today:

1. **The animal kingdom**

   - The birds in the sky
   - The animals that roam the Earth
   - The fish in the sea

2. **The mineral kingdom**

   - Gold
   - Metal
   - Precious gems
   - Oil

3. **The vegetable kingdom**

   - Plants with flowers (these reproduce with seeds)
   - Plants without flowers (these reproduce without seeds)

4. **The kingdom of the stars**

   - Terrestrial type planets
   - Gaseous planets

   The solar system is divided into:

   - Interior planets
   - Exterior planets

5. **The kingdom of mankind**

The kingdom of men is composed of the various governments previously described. In addition, we have countries which are ruled by royal families.

6. **The kingdom of darkness**

- Satan
- Demons or fallen angels

7. **The Kingdom of God**

- Sovereign
- Eternal
- Jesus is King and the head
- Man is a citizen of this Kingdom and the executor of the King's will on Earth
- Angels are warriors, intercessors, and ministering beings

The Kingdom of God governs over every kingdom on Earth with supreme authority.

"¹⁷This decision is by the decree of the watchers, and the sentence by the word of the holy ones, in order that the living may know that the Most High rules in the kingdom of men, gives it to whomever He will, and sets over it the lowest of men." Daniel 4.17

The priority is to seek the Kingdom of God and its righteousness.

"³³But seek (aim at and strive after) first of all His Kingdom and His righteousness (His way of doing and being right), and then all these things taken together will be given you besides." Matthew 6.33— AMP

Illustration: Most people worry about money without realizing that money belongs to the vegetable kingdom. Therefore, why allow the kingdom of leaves—foliage and vegetation—to govern us? Why not seek the sovereign Kingdom of God and allow the other kingdoms to be added unto us?

Jesus taught us to passionately seek the Kingdom of God and its righteousness before material wealth. Our business ventures, jobs, food, drink, wealth, position, fame, or studies should never be our number one priority—that place should be reserved for the Kingdom of Heaven. When the Kingdom is a priority in our lives, everything we need, want, or desire will be added to us, including longevity.

What is the Kingdom of God?

In Greek, the word for **Kingdom** is the word *basileia* which means: royal power, kingship, dominion, or rule. Respectively, we can say that the Kingdom of God is a divine royal power or government. It is not a physical place, person, or thing; it is justice, peace, and joy. It is a jurisdiction that encloses all creation; exercising absolute influence over every inhabitant of the Earth.

> The establishment of the Kingdom
> extends God's virtues and changes
> the atmosphere, everywhere.

How does the Kingdom of God enforce its government?

The Kingdom of God is invisible; thus, governing the visible world from the invisible spiritual realm. This government uses the physical aspect of man to govern on Earth—the visible creation of God. Although the Lord is invisible to the human eye, He is more real than the world we see and feel every day. Just because we do not *see* God or His Kingdom, it does not mean they are inexistent. The Kingdom of God is an invisible spiritual government with a constitution; making it a legal form of government with legal authority; therefore, able to exercise justice.

The Kingdom of God: Is it a physical place?

The Kingdom of God is not a tangible place with buildings or streets. It is a sphere of relationships between God and man, and among men; moreover, this realm is undoubtedly governed by God. The Kingdom is a relationship of total obedience that travels upward from man to God; it is an absolute benevolent dictatorship exercised through divine fatherhood.

According to Jesus, what is the definition of the Kingdom?

"¹⁰Your kingdom come. Your will be done on Earth as it is in heaven."
Matthew 6.10

Jesus taught us to pray for the Kingdom to be established on Earth. He connects this invisible government with the visible through the affirmation of man because He is the one with authority on Earth. On that account, His Kingdom is established anywhere the will of God is completely carried out. According to Jesus, the Kingdom of God is: completely doing and obeying His will on Earth, as it is carried out and obeyed in heaven.

How is the will of God carried out in heaven?

In heaven, the will of God is established through a totalitarian form of government and absolute obedience to the supreme authority of God. In heaven, there is only one will, that of King Jesus, to which all citizens fully respond and obey without question. The answer is always "Yes Sir!" This could be interpreted as bondage or fierce control, but it is not. The Kingdom of God is not led by democracy but by theocracy, operating equally in every sphere: in heaven, on Earth, and the whole universe.

When we willingly obey the laws of the Kingdom, we find complete freedom that no manmade government—a system led by mere humans—can provide. Rather, the will of God is held together by three virtues: It is *good* because it guides towards something good; it is *pleasurable* because it is pleasing to the body, soul, and spirit; and, it is *perfect* because it is the best thing that could happen to man— resulting in his happiness. When we discover this freedom, we gain full conviction that there is no need or desire to change it.

The Kingdom of God is doing the King's will,
on Earth as it is in heaven.
This brings peace and joy to all.

However, when we radically obey an ideological proposal, such as Socialism, Capitalism, or Third Way, the end result is bondage because no government led by man is perfect, complete, or apt to govern man into freedom.

Governments led by men employ everything within their power to govern its citizens with justice, but this becomes difficult to accomplish because they are dealing with fallible systems based on laws and principles that were created by imperfect men; hence, we (the people of God) are compelled to establish the government of God in every nation of the world. Accordingly, men governed by the principles, laws, and mentality of the Kingdom of God are able to transform families, cities, and nations for the best.

How does God carry out His will on Earth, as it is in heaven?

From the beginning, God's plan was that He would govern through a man; a human being in a physical body who would choose to establish His will in this earthly sphere.

"⁴What is man that You are mindful of him, and the son of man that You visit him? ⁵For You have made him a little lower than the angels, and You have crowned him with glory and honor. ⁶You have made him to have dominion over the works of Your hands; you have put all things under his feet." Psalms 8.4-6

God placed Adam and Eve in this position; able to govern over His creation with the authority delegated by Him. However, this authority would be contingent upon their loyalty in choosing to stay subject to His will and government.

God cannot establish His Kingdom or carry out His will on Earth without man's cooperation; not because He lacks the ability or power to do it but because He *chose* it to be this way, since the beginning of time. Remember, He does not violate His word or justice. The government of God has laws that must be obeyed; it has an individual and collective will to which all men must be subject to. He leads by example; therefore, being the first to submit to His laws. However, none of this can be carried out on Earth if there is a shortage of men and women willing to obey God and His government.

There are certain words used in Scripture that make reference to the word, *govern*, these are: dominion, lordship, restrain, or reign; all are synonyms for this word. In short, the Kingdom of God is the divine government in which He governs completely; it is not a physical place but a jurisdiction of relationships. It is an invisible government subject to the will of the King who rules in a totalitarian way. However, keep in mind the difference that exists between totalitarianism birthed on Earth and the one birthed in heaven. Earthly systems of government, such as communism, the Nazi regime, and others, invariably represent bondage because in God's original design, man was not created to govern man.

Consequently, every time the Kingdom of God is mentioned, a declaration of war is made against the kingdom of darkness; this, because the latter has taken over the territories that belong to the government of God. Nevertheless, when man submits to God's Kingdom and carries out the will of its King, the kingdom or government of darkness trembles because it realizes its time is up and has to leave that territory.

Satan's Kingdom operates only where
the divine government has not been established.

The Kingdom of God represents complete order, authority, and the will of God implanted in a territory. It is an invasive and powerful force that removes and replaces the kingdom of Satan, as light up-roots and replaces darkness.

Another key point we must understand is that Satan's government operates under the same laws as the Kingdom of God. In other words, it can only be established on Earth by man. Satan is a spirit, and as such, he does not have the ability or right to directly operate in the material world; thus, leaving all its power in the hands of the only spiritual being that has a physical body: man. Man is the only being who can decide which kingdom will govern his life. Man chooses to which kingdom he will align his will and freedom of choice. Are you willing to become that man or woman who chooses to establish the Kingdom of God on Earth? Are you willing to submit and obey its laws? Or do you prefer to establish and extend Satan's kingdom?

What type of kingdom or government belongs to God?

Now we will learn a few of the predominant characteristics of the Kingdom which will reveal what type of government God has in heaven:

❖ **It is a Kingdom that cannot be shaken**

"28Therefore, since we are receiving a Kingdom which cannot be shaken, let us have grace, by which we may serve God acceptably with reverence and godly fear." Hebrews 12.28

Today, everything is being shaken: the physical and spiritual worlds and the political and religious arenas. However, in the midst of all this shaking, the Kingdom of God remains firm and unshakeable; it is a secure anchor to our soul. The Kingdom of God is eternal; it never changes or falters.

❖ **It governs all human kingdoms or governments**

"12Both riches and honor come from You, and You reign over all. In Your hand is power and might; in Your hand it is to make great and to give strength to all." 1 Chronicles 29.12

As previously mentioned, the six existing kingdoms are under the influence of the Kingdom of God, regardless of whether its members believe that life begins and ends in that particular kingdom. However, the good news about the Kingdom of God is that it is supreme, the most high, and one that governs above every kingdom in the world, whether they know it or not.

"¹⁹The LORD has established His throne in heaven, and His kingdom rules over all." Psalms 103.19

When we think with the mentality of the Kingdom of God, we live beyond the laws established by other kingdoms because its way of thinking, laws, and order, are superior to any system established by man.

❖ **The Kingdom of God operates under the principles of a clearly defined executive head**

There is only one God, and He manifests Himself in three people: Father, Son, and Holy Spirit. They are of one mind, one heart, one intention, one purpose, one passion, and one destiny. Therefore, the Father's position as the executive head does not make Him more God than the Son or the Holy Spirit.

"⁶For to us a Child is born, to us a Son is given; and the government shall be upon His shoulder, and His name shall be called Wonderful Counselor, Mighty God, Everlasting Father [of Eternity], Prince of Peace. ⁷Of the increase of His government and of peace there shall be no end, upon the throne of David and over His Kingdom, to establish it and to uphold it with justice and with righteousness from the [latter] time forth, even forevermore. The zeal of the Lord of hosts will perform this." Isaiah 9.6, 7—AMP

The first thing God said concerning His Son was that His government would be upon His shoulder. If you reread this verse, you will notice that government and peace go together. Wherever the government of God is not established, there is no peace because peace can only be felt under a divine system. This is the reason why the victories in war times can only be secured when the right government is established.

There is no peace without the government of God
because peace only comes where this divine system
has been established.

In essence, the Kingdom of God operates under a plurality of government. In other words, it is made up of many individuals who are led by one executive head that has been clearly defined. In this Kingdom, there are no committees. Governments led by committees or tyrants are easy to rule. However, in both, mistakes are made that eventually lead to chaos and anarchy. In the Holy Trinity, God the Father is the head. In the church, Jesus is the head; in the local church, the pastor is the head; in the family, the man is the head. And yet, in all of these, it is important for the head to be both, father and servant, because that is the only way an effective government can be carried out.

❖ **It is a sovereign Kingdom with absolute authority**

The government of God is a sovereign Kingdom with one will and one absolute and defined authority; it is always right—it never makes mistakes.

"³How great are His signs, and how mighty His wonders! His Kingdom is an everlasting kingdom, and His dominion is from generation to generation." Daniel 4.3

❖ **The Kingdom is ruled by a sovereign God: from eternity to eternity**

"¹⁵...which He will manifest in His own time, He who is the blessed and only Potentate, the King of kings and Lord of lords, ¹⁶who alone has immortality, dwelling in unapproachable light, whom no man has seen or can see, to whom be honor and everlasting power. Amen" 1 Timothy 6.15, 16

❖ **The Kingdom is sovereign: It does and dictates as it sees fit and when it sees fit.**

Praise God! The word **sovereign** is the Greek word *despotes*, which means: master and lord; an absolute governor who imposes absolute and supreme authority. The Spanish word *déspota*—absolute ruler—comes from this Greek word and it means: a tyrant or ruler who governs with supreme and absolute authority. Contrary to the dictatorship of man, the Kingdom is benevolent and completely void of selfishness. God does not govern us with abuse or punishment but with love and through His fatherhood.

Now that we know the characteristics of the Kingdom and how its government operates, we can enjoy the resources and benefits available under its authority. Our trust lies in knowing that it operates for our own good; to bring us peace, well-being, and above all, freedom!

Once we understand what it is, what is our responsibility with the Kingdom or government of God? Before knowing the existence of God's Kingdom, we lived independently of it. But now that we have accepted Jesus and learned how beneficial it is to be in His perfect will and the protection of His government, we ought to develop distinct attitudes which help us stand strong and grow in Him, and Him in us:

- **Surrender our will.**

We must allow the Kingdom to govern us; in doing so, His will can be carried out in us.

- **See the Kingdom.**

The only way to see the invisible government of God is to be born again. Our rebirth is the entry way for those who want to see the Kingdom manifest in their lives.

"³Jesus answered him, I assure you, most solemnly I tell you, that unless a person is born again (anew, from above), he cannot ever see (know, be acquainted with, and experience) the Kingdom of God."
John 3.3—AMP

- **Believe in the Kingdom.**

The word, **believe,** literally means to be persuaded; to trust; to lean on. Jesus said it is not enough to talk about the Kingdom or use its language but also to believe in it.

How do we believe in the Kingdom?

We believe in the existence of the Kingdom by faith, and for this to happen we must believe that it is the government of God; believe it is the total divine order, authority, and absolute will of God. We must believe it is the answer to all of man's needs. The answers we need are not found in religion because it fails to give man what it needs—only the government of God can supply the needs or necessities of mankind.

- **Preach the Kingdom**

"²He sent them to preach the kingdom of God and to heal the sick." Luke 9.2

The word for *preach* is the Greek word *kerusso* which means: to proclaim publicly, after the manner of a messenger, always with the suggestion of formality, gravity, and an authority which must be listened to and obeyed; to proclaim out loud and in public up to the point that it offends. We must preach the Kingdom everywhere we go: at the store, in the office, in the warehouse, in school, in our universities. We must proclaim the Kingdom of God from our daily pulpit. In other words, we must proclaim His Word everywhere, at all times, and to all people.

- **Extend the Kingdom.**

The only way to make the Kingdom of God advance on Earth is by force. We cannot be passive about it because there will always be conflict between the Kingdom of God and the kingdom of darkness. For this reason, we must always be available and willing to obey so that we may extend His Kingdom no matter where God sends us.

We must surrender our will to God
and carry out our responsibility to see the Kingdom,
believe in it, preach it, and extend it.

Chapter 3

THE RIGHTEOUSNESS OF THE KINGDOM OF GOD

The message Jesus proclaimed throughout the gospels always centered on the *Kingdom of God* and its *righteousness*; everything He mentioned was centered on these two subjects. He would begin talking on the Kingdom and continue teaching about righteousness—the most essential element within the government of God. For this reason, it is extremely important to understand the significance of what these mean and practice it in our daily lives.

During the days of Jesus, the righteousness practiced by the Jews was based on the law, service in the temple, and through acts of love and kindness. The Jews practiced an external form of righteousness—they prayed in the marketplace and gave their offerings so people could see them; they would toot their own horn, per say, to ensure recognition. Jesus, on the other hand, presented the righteousness of the heart which comes from a circumcised heart that is transformed and renewed as a consequence of believing in Him. Many people today practice the Pharisaic form of righteousness: They give with superficial motives, to "look good", they pray when they are guaranteed to be seen, they announce their fasting and generosity hoping to be recognized, and so forth. This is not the type of righteousness that operates in the Kingdom, for Kingdom righteousness is one that is birthed in a heart that is in line with the heart of God.

The justice practiced by the Pharisees
does not operate in the Kingdom.
Justice can only be executed
by one who has a heart
aligned with God's heart.

"¹Take heed that you do not do your charitable deeds before men, to be seen by them. Otherwise you have no reward from your Father in heaven."
Matthew 6.1

What is Kingdom righteousness?

The word **righteous**, in Hebrew and Greek, has countless meanings, and all coincide with each other. To discover and understand the meaning of this word at a deeper level, we need to study its several synonyms which appear in the Old and New Testament. Furthermore, as this chapter develops, we will go deeper into the meaning of each word.

In Hebrew, the words for *righteousness* are: *mishpat, tsedeq,* and *tsedaqah;* in Greek, they are: *dikaiosyne, ekdikesis, dikaios, eleemosune* and *krisis.* When we join the meanings of these words, the result is the complete spectrum of what this concept entails:

Righteousness: rights; to vindicate the cause of; prosperity; rectitude; vindication; cause; an attribute of God to be impartial and govern with fairness; salvation; moral rectitude; to absolve; to be in order to do; to justify; works of righteousness; fairness of character; holy character; execute vengeance or judgment; compassion exercised towards the needy; judgment; condemnation; and retribution. When we read these Biblical definitions, we find that the righteousness of the Kingdom of God has five great meanings; there are many more, but these are used most often in both the Old and New Testament.

1. The righteousness of God is for the salvation of mankind.

One meaning of *righteousness* is: salvation; to be justified; to be absolved of sins; to be absolved. Before the arrival of Jesus on Earth, the entire human race was in bondage to sin and condemned to eternal damnation. The book of Isaiah narrated the condemnation of mankind. In those days, Israel had enjoyed years of increased economic prosperity along with a serious spiritual and moral decline. Idolatry to pagan gods was commonplace. Moreover, the rich were oppressing the poor, women failed to care for their families to follow after the desires of their flesh, many of God's prophets and priests had surrendered to drunkenness and worldly pleasures, and masters oppressed their labor force, the poor, and the widow. The rich were enjoying the benefits of their prosperity, practiced religious acts, kept the liturgy, and observed the established religious celebrations, but their hearts were far from God. Their actions and conduct were displeasing before the eyes of the Lord. For this reason, He said their righteousness was like filthy rags and sent them the prophet Isaiah with a message of repentance, salvation, and restoration.

Idolatry and worship to pagan gods
has nothing to do with divine justice; rather,
it brings the judgment of God over a region.

In the days of Jesus, the same was taking place as in the days of the prophet Isaiah; there was no justice—righteousness—for the orphan, the foreigner was not given any help, and the needs of the widow were not taken care of. The people presented a rebellious attitude towards the Lord and had turned their worship toward pagan gods and sought only to increase their wealth. Lies, evil, and iniquity had taken over the hearts of the people, and this was very displeasing before God. Justice or righteousness and rights had dissipated.

"¹⁴Justice is turned back, and righteousness stands afar off; for truth is fallen in the street, and equity cannot enter. ¹⁵So truth fails, and he who departs from evil makes himself a prey." Isaiah 59.14, 15

What took place in the days of the prophet Isaiah also took place during the days of Jesus. God was always looking for a righteous man; one willing to do works of righteousness and restore the rights of the people, but He could not find one.

"¹⁶He saw that there was no man, and wondered that there was no intercessor; therefore His own arm brought salvation for Him; and His own righteousness, it sustained Him." Isaiah 59.16

What was God's next move when He could not find one man or woman who could do the works of righteousness?

"¹⁷For He put on righteousness as a breastplate, and a helmet of salvation on His head; He put on the garments of vengeance for clothing, and was clad with zeal as a cloak. ¹⁸According to their deeds, accordingly He will repay, fury to His adversaries, recompense to His enemies; the coastlands He will fully repay." Isaiah 59.17, 18

God became man in the person of His Son Jesus, not only to bring justice and salvation but also to restore the rights of the people of Israel and of every human being. Jesus, the righteous God-man who came to this Earth, had two great virtues which are indispensable when trying to restore justice or righteousness:

"⁷You love righteousness and hate wickedness; therefore God, Your God, has anointed You with the oil of gladness more than Your companions." Psalms 45.7

❖ **Jesus loved righteousness.**

More than a desire, it is a passion to see restored the rights of the people and lead the lost to salvation; an unquenchable passion that burned in Jesus. He had a hunger and thirst to see their rights prevail.

❖ **Jesus hated iniquity.**

One cannot be just if evil, wickedness, lying, deceitfulness, pride, and arrogance are not hated. Iniquity is exactly opposite to righteousness; it means to be unjust or to misconstrue the rights of others.

As we read in the book of Isaiah, Jesus was clothed in a mantle of righteousness, and with it, He brought salvation to mankind who was lost in sin, hopelessness, and condemned to death and destruction. Jesus became a man, lived 33 and a half years on Earth. During this time, He walked in perfect obedience, leading Him to the cross where He willingly took upon Himself the sins, rebellions, iniquity, sickness, and pain of all mankind. He paid the price for our sin, at the cross. He died and was buried, but on the third day, He was raised with power and authority to bring righteousness to all those who, through faith, choose to believe in Him.

The first aspect of righteousness concerns His ability to be just with sinners; this is something He had already dealt with before the foundation of the world. God loves man, but he sinned, and His sense of justice obligates Him to deal with man in a perfect and righteous way; this, because the foundation of His government *is* justice. God has to deal with man within the divine standards: perfection and holiness. He cannot tolerate iniquity, He hates sin, and He never lies. God cannot compromise the truth simply out of love for the people because His righteousness does not allow Him to do so. He does not *choose* to be righteous—He *is* just and righteous; it is a fixed and unchanging character trait in Him.

When God justifies us,
it is the legal declaration that we are just.

For lack of a better word, there is certain tension between His perfect love and righteousness; to this, we must also add another great attribute of God, His holiness. Everyone who approaches Him must be holy. The anger of God goes against injustice and ungodliness—although His love and mercy want to manifest, He must act with the righteousness He sees fit and proceed within His norms of sanctity.

What was the condition of man and the world before Christ?

"[11]There is none who understands; there is none who seeks after God. [12]They have all turned aside; they have together become unprofitable;

there is none who does good, no, not one." "23...for all have sinned and fall short of the glory of God..." Romans 3.11, 12, 23

All men have sinned. If it were not for God's mercy, our future would be confirmed in hell. If anyone were to cry out for righteousness, God would answer accordingly and pass down His righteous decree. In doing so, we would still be confined to the destiny we have earned—hell—because not one of us has been, is, or ever will be good. No one can stand before God and say, "I deserve to go to heaven" because all men have sinned and fallen short of the glory of God. In view of that, He sent His Son, Jesus, who through the shedding of His blood and our faith in Him, would reconcile humanity with God. This was the viable solution for God to manifest His righteousness.

"25...whom God set forth as a propitiation by His blood, through faith, to demonstrate His righteousness, because in His forbearance God had passed over the sins that were previously committed..."
Romans 3.25

The word **propitiation** means: to satisfy, pay, or justify. Jesus, through His sacrifice, justified the anger of God. He paid the price to satisfy God's wrath against the sin of man.

Illustration: Imagine reading on the front page of every newspaper about a judge in your city who is holding a public trial; the accused, without a shadow of a doubt, is guilty. Righteousness is being demanded and judgment must be passed in public. During the trial, the evidence presented successfully accuses the defendant and demands justice, but suddenly, the judge steps down from his place of honor, removes the garment he is wearing, which identifies him as the judge, and declares before the witnesses and district attorney: "I will pay the debt. I will assume his guilt. I make myself guilty; judge me; I will pay the punishment on his behalf." Stop for a moment and imagine how surprised the people are to see that the one who should be passing the "guilty" verdict takes *upon himself* the guilt of the accused and accepts the punishment for the defendant's crimes.

This example is a precise illustration of what Jesus did for us: He died publicly. He was judged and humbled Himself in public before the principalities and strongholds, before the angels and the people, and paid the debt so that *we* could be justified and found righteous.

There are two types of righteousness:

❖ **Righteousness that comes through works**

Righteousness, through the law, is accomplished by works. These are performed to gain acceptance and merit before God. However, no one can be justified through these no matter how much we believe, fast, or give to our neighbors; regardless of how much we read the Bible or how much "good" we do. This is not to say that good works are obsolete—we must continue to do good works—not to win the favor of God but because we love Him and our neighbors. In other words, we must perform good works as a reflection of the fruit of the Spirit in our lives.

Justice by works is powerless before God;
only faith in Jesus has the power to justify us.

❖ **Righteousness through faith**

Righteousness through faith "speaks" loud and clear. The difference between righteousness by works and righteousness through faith is that no one could ever be justified through works; however, through faith in Jesus, we become the righteousness of Christ.

"⁶But the righteousness of faith speaks in this way, "Do not say in your heart, 'Who will ascend into heaven?'" (that is, to bring Christ down from above) ⁷or, "'Who will descend into the abyss?'" (that is, to bring Christ up from the dead). ⁸But what does it say? "The word is near you, in your mouth and in your heart" (that is,

the word of faith which we preach): ⁹that if you confess with your mouth the Lord Jesus and believe in your heart that God has raised Him from the dead, you will be saved. ¹⁰For with the heart one believes unto righteousness and with the mouth confession is made unto salvation." Romans 10.6-10

We must confess with our mouths and believe in our hearts that Jesus is the Son of God; it is only in that confession that we are justified and become righteous, like Jesus. Believing in and accepting Jesus for who He is and what He has done, attributes His justice and righteousness in us without us having to do anything else. Of course, after this takes place, we will be lead through the path of righteousness which is in us through faith. Further, we are to endure the process, live it, and experience it; this constitutes the experiences of righteousness.

The righteousness of God is revealed through faith; it is *then* that we become like Jesus and begin to act like Him. This is the gospel of the Kingdom. Paul taught that he who confesses with his mouth that Jesus Christ is Lord will be saved. In Greek, the word for *Lord* is *kyrios*; this title is given to one who has legal rights over the life and death of others. We must confess that Jesus is *the* Lord—the absolute authority over our lives. Also, we must believe, wholeheartedly, that He was raised from the dead—*then*, God's righteousness will be attributed to us, through faith.

Righteousness that comes through faith has two facets:

- **Righteousness that is attributed.** This type of righteousness was given or attributed to us *before* manifesting in our lives and without us having to earn it; the only condition to receiving it is to believe in Jesus.

- **Righteousness that is imparted.** Imparted righteousness is manifested so that we may experience His righteousness in us, every day; it leads us to righteous living.

This is a matter of faith, not works, which comes through a close relationship with God. Once we receive this attribute, His righteousness becomes a daily experience that is imparted by the Holy Spirit who now dwells in us. God increases our faith and takes us from righteousness to righteousness and from glory to glory, until we become the image of Christ.

In going from *attributed* righteousness to having it *imparted*, there are various levels one must experience that can only be accomplished through faith. As we confess righteousness, it becomes a reality in our lives; as our faith increases, we receive more impartation, and a greater level of moral uprightness, sanctity, and maturity is added to our lives. We do not have to *do (deeds)* anything to become righteous or holy, but we do have to *believe* and *confess*. To confess righteousness is to speak what God speaks, to believe what God believes, and to allow the Holy Spirit to guide our lives. When the righteousness of the Kingdom ends its transforming work in us, we will be as righteous as Jesus, praise God!

Illustration: There is a huge difference between having your boss usher you into his office on payday to tell you, "I have a gift for you, here is your paycheck."—to which you reply, "This is not a gift, I had to work hard to earn it;" versus, you having been out of work for a month and your boss tells you, "I give you this gift, your regular paycheck, even though you did not work for it." Similarly, God can take our disasters and turn them into victories, but this can only be accomplished if we believe and accept His righteousness through faith and not by trying to earn them through works.

If one person believes that God can justify him,
then he can believe for the entire world.

How does Jesus justify us?

"¹Therefore, having been justified by faith, we have peace with God through our Lord Jesus Christ." Romans 5.1

Those who believe, through faith in Christ, are justified; our faults, sins, and iniquity are absolved and the righteousness of Christ is attributed to us; this is what took place with the father of our faith, Abraham. He was justified by faith, not by works; and in the same way, righteousness was attributed to him.

"⁶And he believed in the LORD, and He accounted it to him for right-eousness." Genesis 15.6

It is wonderful to know that God paid the price according to our works; the punishment and condemnation that would be over us were placed upon His Son, Jesus. He carried our iniquity on His back. We were not justified by works but by grace and through faith in Him and His redeeming work; in doing this, we are able to become men and women of great moral recti-tude with a character that is holy, in the likeness of Him who redeemed us.

"²⁹If you know that He is righteous, you know that everyone who prac-tices righteousness is born of Him." 1 John 2.29

God declared us to be righteous, just, clean, justified, absolved of all guilt and sin, but He did not justify us by our works because that would be impossible to accomplish in our own strength. If it were so, salvation would not come by *grace*. We were justified by faith— declared righteous through our faith in Christ and His grace. This is the principle behind God's manifestation of His righteousness: To save man so he can be transformed into a righteous man; one who is just, honest, and upright—one who practices the righteousness of the Kingdom. If we bring His righteousness to Earth we, in fact, establish the Kingdom if God.

2. **The righteousness of the Kingdom means to be upright, to be in right standing, morally right, and blameless before God.**

The manifestation of God's righteousness, in this case, means:

❖ To be upright, blameless, and proper according to a standard or person.

❖ Righteousness is the quality of life or righteous behavior; to live morally correct or in rectitude before God.

God does not choose to be just.
He *is* justice.

Illustration: Government leaders pass norms and laws that must be observed by their citizens. The government's view of our righteousness is directly related to our obedience and submission to the city laws; in their eyes, we are recognized as righteous citizens because we obey.

As far as we are concerned, everything started taking place when we repented for living outside the laws and regulations of God's government. Consequently, our new-found obedience towards His laws now allows us to be called "righteous." This does not mean we won that righteousness by performing good works; we are righteous because God made us righteous. Furthermore, we are now just, upright, and blameless before the eyes of God, just like Jesus. We can behave in an upright manner before God because righteousness has been instilled in us which leads to experience imparted righteousness. These things can only take place through faith and not by any works we may perform.

If I consider myself to be a righteous person, it means that everything I do is correct before the eyes of God. I follow God's standards and not the world's because my righteousness or rectitude is not based on laws, regulations, or principles of government. When man is governed according to standards not in line with the Kingdom, he steps outside God's Kingdom and becomes unrighteous. Similarly, when a person does not practice a correct, upright, or just lifestyle before the eyes of God, that person becomes afraid or even terrified to be in His presence—as it happened to Adam. Although, it is terrible to be improper or to go before the presence of God as one who is unjust, it is worst to live eternity without God.

If we are to live in God's presence, we must practice a life that is just, upright, and correct, every day—extending this lifestyle in everything we do and think. Under the law, no one can be righteous, but under grace, it is possible. God attributed His righteousness unto us so that we could live in it through faith.

When man receives the Kingdom of God, he begins to experience a commanding desire to be righteous; thus, if you do not want to be righteous, upright, or morally blameless, if this lifestyle is unappealing to you, then you cannot live within the government of God which is founded in righteousness.

The meaning of righteousness is to live upright, correct, and morally blameless. When we receive the revelation of this meaning, we experience the compelling desire to live in His righteousness, like that of a man who thirsts and seeks water. This enables us to increase our faith, and live from righteousness to righteousness; thus, making the Kingdom of God a reality in us. Then, and only then, our priority becomes seeking the Kingdom of God and its righteousness.

In other words, no one can experience true righteousness until he is birthed from the Just One. Jesus said it another way: "No one can see nor enter the Kingdom of God unless he is born again." If the heart of man does not change with the righteousness of God, he can never live in peace with himself or others. The righteousness of the Kingdom must be applied, lived, and executed with a pure and transformed heart. Otherwise, what he experiences will be "good intentions" but not righteousness. True righteousness comes from God, and if it is not attributed to man, the only thing man can produce are filthy rags—works of the flesh performed for the purpose of gaining merit or acknowledgment before God, which are not acceptable to Him. Genuine righteousness can only come from God and His Kingdom.

"¹⁴Righteousness and justice are the foundation of Your throne; mercy and truth go before Your face." Psalms 89.14

———————— ❦ ————————
Good intentions
are not enough to transform cities.
———————— ❦ ————————

The righteousness of God is the legal declaration that we are righteous. Today, millions of worldly and Christian leaders—in government, church, business, and family—are trying to be righteous in their own strength by taking into account only how *they* think things should be. However, since righteousness belongs to God, their efforts are futile and nothing happens. People, whose hearts remain unchanged by the righteousness of the Kingdom, merely have "good intentions," but this is not enough to transform a city, state, nation, or family. They need to have a personal encounter with the righteous God who imparts righteousness; then, they need to be justified before they can exercise the righteousness they received. The first manifestation of righteousness is the salvation of the lost and the vindication of His cause. Remember, salvation also includes: prosperity, inner healing, deliverance, peace, and the fulfillment of all things.

3. **The righteousness of the Kingdom restores justice and causes rights to prevail.**

"⁶The LORD executes righteousness and justice for all who are oppressed." Psalms 103.6

For justice to prevail, we must be full of the righteousness of God; once it is recognized, it must be shared with others. We are to ensure God's righteousness is also exposed to those who live outside of God's protection and justice.

Today, many organizations fight for their individual rights: the gay community fights for rights, women endorse their feminist outlook, and religious extremist fight for their rights to be heard. Likewise, many other groups fight for what they believe to be right even though their "rights" do not derive from the righteousness of the Kingdom of God but of their personal sense of righteousness—they come from a lascivious, sinful, and selfish behavior. They fight to remove Biblical norms from government, schools, and even churches in order to satisfy decadent desires while still considering them "righteous." They change the law or diminish the rights of individuals or groups, not for the purpose of helping or serving, but rather, to propagate personal lifestyles and impose them on others at the expense of leading themselves and others to self-destruction.

———————— ⚜ ————————
Fighting for a just cause doesn't necessarily please God.
He looks at the intention of your heart not the work of your hands.
———————— ⚜ ————————

Some people may do the wrong thing for the right reasons. Others do what they do because their hearts are corrupted or because they need to fight for a cause that will make a difference in this world. It is both disappointing and unfortunate that people who fight to make a difference do so for the wrong reasons.

We were not placed on this Earth to follow a personal agenda or to try and establish a personal sense of justice. We are here to carry out the will of God and execute His righteousness. In other words, we are here to fight for the rights that the Kingdom of God attributes to those unable to care for themselves or who do not have the necessary resources. These are just and righteous reasons to fight for. Jesus declared the following:

"⁶Blessed and fortunate and happy and spiritually prosperous (in that state in which the born-again child of God enjoys His favor and salvation) are those who hunger and thirst for righteousness (uprightness and right standing with God), for they shall be completely satisfied!"
Matthew 5.6—AMP

Today, God searches for men and women who love justice and hate iniquity; people who want to fight for the rights of the impoverished, the widow, the needy, and the foreigner. Modern society is on the decline—losing its moral values to the point where men fight more for the rights of animals (i.e. dogs, whales, birds, lions, etc.) than rights for human beings to live. Moreover, society goes as far as compensating them with trophies and promotions, while those who defend the right for a child to live are condemned, forgotten, or their case is lost in red tape and bureaucracy. Because animal rights activists are determined to fight for animal rights, when an animal is killed, the culprit is fined and sometimes imprisoned.

If your heart is pure,
your works will be just.

Why are so few fighting for the rights of the unborn? Why are people unwilling to stand up and let their voices be heard as they fight for the rights of these little ones to live? Why are so few willing to be counted among the people who will fight for the rights of the unborn babies to live? Why are so few fighting against abortion?[1]

Doctors who perform abortions are not imprisoned, but people who kill animals are. What has more worth in today's society?—a dog or a person that is growing in its mother's womb? Thousands of children cry out for justice; they want their rights protected and respected. Who will stand up for justice and do whatever it takes to make their rights prevail?[2]

There must be at least one person hungry and thirsty for righteousness; someone who hates iniquity and is willing to fight for

---

[1] An average of 50 million abortions per year are performed around the world— https://www.cia.gov/library/publications/the-world-factbook/docs/notesanddefs.html.

[2] Today, the traffic of human lives is approximately 800,000 per year; most are women and children who are sold for sexual slavery and forced labor. https://www.cia.gov/library/publications/the-world-factbook/docs/notesanddefs.html

those who are defenseless to have rights that will prevail. For every injustice, there must be someone who is righteous—a citizen of the Kingdom willing to fight for the rights of the defenseless. Jesus, the righteous One, came to establish His Kingdom and righteousness among men. He came to restore the rights of the weak; making the weak prevail and fighting for this to be accomplished according to Kingdom righteousness.

Millions of people—men, women, young people, and children—in this nation and around the world are crying out for someone willing to stand up and fight on their behalf. Millions of women who are emotionally and physically abused by their husbands or employers are crying out for justice; others cry out for justice because their salaries are below the pay rate that men receive for performing the same job; others cry out for their rights to be heard in the church because no one believes they are called into ministry. Women everywhere are crying out to be treated fairly. In some countries and cultures, women are treated as dogs; as second class citizens. They are not treated equally or fairly nor do they have the same privileges as men—neither in society nor in their respective religions.[3]

The question that immediately comes to mind is: "Why is this taking place if God created everyone equal and in His image and likeness?" Someone needs to stand up and fight for justice, such as: women rights to prevail against injustice. Furthermore, it is a fight to protect God's intended plan for His creation; to protect it from perversion or destruction. If God created gifted women with abilities and fortitude to establish His Kingdom on Earth, who are we to deny them that right? To do such a thing is equal to denying His wisdom or as if we were telling God that He made a mistake.

Today, millions of women are treated like second class citizens. They are abused, rejected, and treated as if their entire value consisted only in being objects created for sexual satisfaction or

---

[3] In the United States, every two minutes a woman is sexually attacked. (2005 National Crime Victimization Survey (PDF 287KB) from the Bureau of Justice Statistics, U.S. Department of Justice.)

THE RIGHTEOUSNESS OF THE KINGDOM OF GOD |

reproduction. Women are hurting; they are being mistreated and abused by male arrogance and by the injustice in a society that is blind to moral values and human needs. Who will stand up and fight for the rights of women?—rights which were given by God?

Today, thousands of children—boys and girls—are being used to endorse pornography, not only in the USA but also around the world; this industry generates more money than any other world-wide.

Illustration: Sometime ago, I saw a television program that showed that in Asia, pagan evil men were buying children (three to five years old) to perform oral sex with them and others. Upon their rescue, the children's faces were marked by the obvious and horrible abuse they had suffered in the hands of their captors. Once again, I was reminded that God has not ended His search for men and women willing to fight for justice and for the rights of children to prevail. Such atrocities are like flaming arrows that pierce the heart of God. He needs men and women willing to fight for the children, so they can enjoy the opportunity to grow healthy, safe, pure, and free from such monstrous abuse.[4]

Millions of impoverished people, widows, and immigrants who have no place to live and who are without resources cry out for their right to eat and provide for their families. Who will fight for their rights? Who will speak out in favor of the foreigner being exploited? Who will fight for the rights of Latin American children around the world who, from the age of five, have worked under the sun's blistering heat and who by the age of nine are performing ardeous labor? (UNICEF revealed that one out of every twelve children under the age of 18 work around the globe, under terrible conditions, and are abused and exploited by others. Approximately, 180 million children under

---

[4] UNICEF estimates that a million children per year are forced into prostitution or used for child pornography. http://www.1.hcdn.gov.ar/folio-cgi-bin/om_isapi.dll?clientID=1026898414&advquery=5665-D-05&infobase=tp.nfo&record= ABD8 &recordswithhits=on&softpage=proyecto

the age of 18 are subjected to hard, forced, and dangerous jobs; they are enslaved, forced to enlist in the army, forced into prostitution, and other illegal activities. Studies show that 97% of children who are exploited live in impoverished countries or third world countries; they also make note that poverty and lack of skills and education force children to enter the world of hard labor and exploitation at a very young age.arduous labor?[5]

Who will speak for the rights of the innocent and imprisoned? Is there no one who thirsts and hungers for justice and righteousness? Is there no one who can help? Who will fight for the people that suffer because they are discriminated for the color of their skin, the language they speak, or their place of birth? Who will fight to establish health benefits, healing, salvation, prosperity, peace, and joy and have them restored from being people lost in their own sin? Where are the men and women who want to provide the answer to injustice and lack of human rights to a society that becomes more corrupt each day? Who will take the gospel of the Kingdom of God and its righteousness to the impoverished, lost, and rejected by society?

Young people are also crying out for a better education. They demand to be heard, to be freed from the pressure and bondage of gangs, alcohol, and drugs. They need someone to stand up for justice and make their rights heard. Many young people who join gangs do so because they never had a mother, father, or family who loved them. Consequently, they are rebellious against God and society. *Someone* needs to rescue them!

Grown men cry out for justice too; men who were sexually abused and rejected by society for the color of their skin; men who

---

[5] UNICEF revealed that one out of every twelve children under the age of 18 work around the globe, under terrible conditions, and are abused and exploited by others. Approximately, 180 million children under the age of 18 are subjected to hard, forced, and dangerous jobs; they are enslaved, forced to enlist in the army, forced into prostitution, and other illegal activities. Studies show that 97% of children who are exploited live in impoverished countries or third world countries; they also make note that children enter the world of hard labor and abuse because of poverty and lack of education.")
http://www.consumer.es/web/es/solidaridad/2005/02/22/117214.php

lost their fatherhood, masculinity, and priesthood. Men are crying out for justice!

The work of Jesus at the cross restored the rights of God's children.

We, God's children, have the right to enjoy salvation, restoration, financial blessings, physical health, deliverance, security, peace, and joy. However, these things cannot be achieved in our own strength but through the redeeming work of Jesus at the Cross. His sacrifice provided us with His justice which justified and restored our rights. We must take the good news of the gospel to those who are oppressed by this society's injustice and help restore them to their proper position in God. We must defend their rights and lead them into life in the Kingdom.

Injustice will continue to operate in our churches, families, homes, businesses, cities, and nations until men and women who thirst and hunger for righteousness, who love to establish the rights of the Kingdom, and who hate iniquity, stand up and make themselves heard. These people must not seek to satisfy their personal needs, but rather, the needs of others. They must refrain from seeking positions within the church, the marketplace, or in government, for *personal* gain. Their efforts must be directed towards restoring the rights and benevolent righteousness of *God*. The world is consumed by people seeking to spread their immoral conduct and sinful lifestyles; when what we truly need is people who seek to benefit their neighbors, to establish justice for the defenseless, and to benefit those who are least capable of doing it for themselves.

What is the reward God offers those who fight for His Kingdom and justice?

"...they shall be completely satisfied!"

God will fill them with the joy and peace that cannot be gained by any other means. Fighting for the rights of others produces a satisfaction that cannot be experienced; even having all the gold or fame in the world cannot measure up to the joy and peace that comes from God.

Illustration: When I travel to Latin America or any other country around the world to hold crusades, I see the stadiums full of thousands of people, many of whom come with sunken eyes caused by depression, sadness, hopelessness, and with the trace of sin in their faces; yet, when they meet Jesus, they are saved and become citizens of the Kingdom of God—the expression on their face changes instantly. The first time I see them, they seem hopeless, but when I return months later, I see them well dressed, serving in church, with joy and happiness on their faces. They were sick and lost in addictions and sin before meeting the Lord, but as soon as they entered the Kingdom, their lives were radically changed and transformed. Not only do they receive salvation but they also walk away physically healed. Their eyes shine with the light of hope and a sense of destiny—that satisfies me and fills my heart more than money, fame, position, or anything else.

Often times, people do not understand why I travel to numerous nations preaching the gospel of the Kingdom. The truth is that I travel because I have great compassion for those who need peace, salvation, and joy. The gospel fulfills these exact needs for those who are willing to receive it. I do not seek money or fame. I am, however, passionate to take the Kingdom of God into their lives so justice can touch them and they can live, not in poverty, but in spiritual and material abundance.

"[11]He shall see the labor of His soul, and be satisfied. By His knowledge My righteous Servant shall justify many, for He shall bear their iniquities." Isaiah 53.11

Jesus left this Earth satisfied. When He was raised, He saw the fruit of His death: the redemption of millions who were spiritually dead. Through His death and resurrection, they received salvation, eternal life, righteousness, peace, joy, and more importantly, restoration of their relationship with the Heavenly Father.

Justice has a redeeming effect
in the heart of man.

Righteousness has a particular effect on the heart. No one who is genuinely born again will feel satisfied until he starts to fight the Kingdom's rights to prevail in his life and the lives of others. Why? Because only then will one experience peace, joy, and salvation to the fullest—this is Kingdom righteousness or God's justice; unlike any manmade righteousness.

"17The work of righteousness will be peace, and the effect of righteousness, quietness and assurance forever."Isaiah 32.17

Do you want to be that man or woman? Are you ready to fight for Kingdom rights to be restored? Are you willing to pay the price to restore justice? Are you willing to suffer persecution to become a voice who speaks in favor of the weak, instead of settling for the *status quo*? Are you willing to suffer persecution for the cause of justice? Are you willing to fight for the rights of children, teens, men, or women who are without resources to do it for themselves? Read the following verse to learn what God asked of Isaiah:

"8Also I heard the voice of the Lord, saying: "Whom shall I send, and who will go for Us?" Then I said, "Here am I! Send me." Isaiah 6.8

God needs your body, mind, soul, and spirit; the talents and resources He gave you so you can go in His name and make the Kingdom's righteousness abound in favor of the needy. We must answer His call, like Isaiah, and make ourselves available to carry out the will of God on Earth.

The righteousness of God is defined as a **cause.** Many have made communism their cause; others have made religion their cause—they strap bombs to their bodies and commit suicide in the name of dead religions. What a waste to die for wicked reasons! Why not live and die for the righteousness of the Kingdom, for the well-being of others, for health, peace, and salvation of others? Would you like to make righteousness and the Kingdom of God your cause to fight for in life? If you do, you will find absolute satisfaction while making a difference in the lives of others.

4. **The righteousness of God is to do works of social justice.**

In Scripture, God teaches that part of His righteousness means to do good works for the well-being of those in need; this is the heart of God. In other words, righteousness is not just preaching the message of salvation but also feeding empty bellies and covering people's nakedness. However, keep in mind that performing works that create social justice are not to be done to win the favor of God. Rather, it is the fruit of righteousness that was instilled within us and sprung into existence after Jesus paid the price at the cross. If we do such things, prior to knowing Jesus—in our own strength and righteousness—those works are nothing more than filthy rags before God. If we do them after being justified by Jesus, then, those works are good and pleasing unto Him. The reason behind this truth is in knowing good works are not performed to receive salvation; rather, they are performed as a *result* of our salvation. They come from a sincere heart that wants to help the needy, not merely to be acknowledged by God.

"17...learn to do good; seek justice, rebuke the oppressor; defend the fatherless, plead for the widow." Isaiah 1.17

In obedience to God's Word, the church should focus, not only on taking care of people's spiritual lives but their physical well-being as well, which include: food, clothing, and shelter; this endorses the meaning of the Kingdom's righteousness into the lives of men. If we say the Kingdom has arrived, but the weak and disabled are without justice, then, the reality is that the Kingdom did not arrive. It may be that His Word arrived, but the Kingdom is yet to be established. Divine righteousness is a result of the Kingdom being established.

"³Defend the poor and fatherless; do justice to the afflicted and needy. ⁴Deliver the poor and needy; free them from the hand of the wicked." Psalms 82.3, 4

Men and women with the heart of God will
cry out for justice on behalf of the weak and vulnerable.

According to this Psalm, David cried out for divine justice, thousands of years before the Kingdom of God was established on Earth. Defending the rights of the weak and defenseless is one way to demonstrate the love of God to those in need; another way is to reach out to the forgotten and rejected by society and those desperately needing to know and feel God's love. God repeats this over and over again in the Old Testament.

"⁶Is this not the fast that I have chosen: to loose the bonds of wickedness, to undo the heavy burdens, to let the oppressed go free, and that you break every yoke? ⁷Is it not to share your bread with the hungry, and that you bring to your house the poor who are cast out; when you see the naked, that you cover him, and not hide yourself from your own flesh?" Isaiah 58.6, 7

Illustration: As a ministry, we work hard to invest money and resources into orphanages in different countries where we can feed, help, and educate homeless children. This project foresees these children will become men and women of integrity. These homes also offer food, clothing, shelter, and natural and spiritual education. We want to leave them the complete inheritance!

Also, at the local level, we feed the hungry, clothe the naked, and established a system in which the people can receive the help they need. Furthermore, every time we travel on a missionary trip, we take food and clothing for the poor because we understand that our duty goes beyond sharing the gospel and meeting the spiritual needs of the people. With food and clothing, we also meet their physical needs. We believe it is impossible to exercise the righteousness of God to its fullest if we fail to exercise social righteousness.

---

*Without works of social righteousness,
the righteousness of the Kingdom is incomplete.*

Likewise, as part of our vision, we are diligently working to establish medical clinics to help the sick; rehabilitation centers for those who suffer with drug addictions; self-help programs for the elderly, young adults, and all who need it; and a legal assessment office where people can inquire on a variety of legal subjects, including advice on immigration policies.

5. God's righteousness governs and judges, impartially.

God is just, even with His enemies.

"8He shall judge the world in righteousness, and He shall administer judgment for the peoples in uprightness." Psalms 9.8

A major problem in society, caused by injustice, is the tendency of people to judge and express their racial opinions. This type of racism discriminates based on social status, the economic level, or the influence they possess. To show and manifest the righteousness of God, on Earth, we must govern and judge without prejudice. We must be just and fair. However, this type of behavior can only be carried out by someone whose heart was changed by God; someone full of God's love and whose character was shaped by Him. We are not only citizens of the Kingdom but also ambassadors of the Kingdom, on Earth. We are called to judge without prejudice and with moral rectitude because when it comes to solving the conflicts that rise in human relationships we are an extension of His justice and righteousness.

"2When the righteous are in authority, the people rejoice; but when a wicked man rules, the people groan." Proverbs 29.2

When a morally upright individual governs a city or nation, the people rejoice because justice is executed according to the principles and laws of the Kingdom of God resulting in judgment without prejudice. On the other hand, when a prejudice and immoral individual governs, everyone suffers. People suffer and cry out for justice because of their hunger, nakedness, unfair treatment, and degradation of moral values. For this reason, prayer for our governmental leaders becomes very important if we are to obtain moral and righteous people to occupy the key positions in government.

The Priority: Seek the Kingdom of God and Its Righteousness

Like in today's society, the priority in Jesus' time was to seek material wealth. If we were to return to the precise moment when Jesus delivered the sermon at the Mount, we would hear the Lord teach the beatitudes. There, He challenged the multitude and disciples to finally change their first priority.

"25Therefore I say to you, do not worry about your life, what you will eat or what you will drink; nor about your body, what you will put on. Is not life more than food and the body more than clothing?" Matthew 6.25

The word **worry** means: to be preoccupied; divided in two; distracted; anxious, tense, or under pressure—worry takes place when the desire to seek material wealth is greater than the desire to live and experience the Kingdom of God and its righteousness.

"26Look at the birds of the air, for they neither sow nor reap nor gather into barns; yet your heavenly Father feeds them. Are you not of more value than they? 27Which of you by worrying can add one cubit to his stature?" Matthew 6.26, 27

In the preceding verse, Jesus teaches that we are worth more than the birds in the air. This means we can rest assured that all of our needs will be met because our Heavenly Father will feed us and supply our every need—more abundantly than what He gives the birds and with greater dedication and care because we are a very special treasure to Him. Jesus also said to take time to consider the flowers in the fields: they do not labor, yet the Lord clothes them. If

He does these things for birds and flowers, how much more will He do for us—His children?

"³¹Therefore do not worry, saying, 'What shall we eat?' or 'What shall we drink?' or 'What shall we wear?' ³²For after all these things the Gentiles seek. For your heavenly Father knows that you need all these things."
Matthew 6.31, 32

People who are not in covenant with God, who have not entered into His Kingdom, and who are not His children, seek jobs, business ventures, pleasures, clothing, new cars, big houses, and/or food, first— these are their priorities. However, our Heavenly Father knows what we need, and He will show us how to meet the desires of our hearts without getting anxious or depressed.

When a person constantly lacks material blessings,
it is a sign that he/she is not seeking
the Kingdom of God and its righteousness.

"³³But seek first the Kingdom of God and His righteousness, and all these things shall be added to you." Matthew 6.33

The first word that leaves the Master's lips is: **seek.** In Greek, the word for *seek* is the word *zeteo* which means: to seek in order to find (by thinking, meditating, reasoning, or to enquire into); to seek or strive after; to seek for or aim at; to seek as in require or demand; to crave or demand something from someone. This word conveys the same idea as that of a man desperately seeking water to quench his thirst.

In Hebrew, it is the word *baqash*: to seek, by any means possible, in praise and worship; to make every effort; to exert oneself or strive for; to desire, demand, inquire, intercede, and beg.

Another word for *seek* is the Hebrew word *darash* which means: to resort to, seek with care, enquire, or require; to consult or enquire of God; to seek deity in prayer and worship; to demand, investigate, ask for, practice, study, follow, or seek with application; to seek God in order to establish a relationship with Him.

The second word Jesus spoke was: **first.** The meaning of this word refers to: priority; what is more essential or necessary; what is more important before the eyes and heart of God. The third word He spoke was: **Kingdom.** In Greek, it is the word *basileia*; it means: royal power, kingship, dominion, or rule. The fourth word was: **righteousness** (as previously discussed in detail).

When we join these four words found in Matthew 6.33 and look at their combined meanings, we can rephrase the verse in the following way:

"But seek, aim at, or strive after, ardently, like someone who is desperate because of his unquenching thirst; worship God and seek carefully and diligently, with every intent and persistence, with determination to find; study the operations of the government, dominium, and supernatural leadership of God and its righteousness. If you do this, rights, morality, uprightness, rectitude, cause, equity, and all other things will be added unto you."

In essence, Jesus said to learn the principles, values, and laws of the Kingdom, alongside its manifestations, signs, and wonders. He also said we should worship and have a personal relationship with the Father; to be determined; passionately desiring His presence, justice, righteousness, and all other virtues. In other words:

"Go and be resolute about seeking the Kingdom. Choose to submit and obey to the government of God. Intercede and cry out so the Kingdom can be established on Earth. Continue to seek out the Kingdom. Endeavor to uphold and maintain your salvation, maturity, and to discover God's purpose. Aim to experience the Kingdom's manifestations so you, too, can be instruments of the same." In essence, it only took Jesus, a few words to deliver the message He was sent to preach on Earth.

"Fight for the salvation of those who live without the Kingdom of God. Study and learn to recognize His Kingdom. Become instruments in God's hands and contribute in the expansion of His Kingdom. Seek justice and righteousness, applying them to your fight for the rights of the disadvantaged who are without the essential resources needed to fight for themselves. Seek to live a moral, faith-filled, and upright life before God. Carry out works of social righteousness. When you seek to do these things—seek the Kingdom of God and its righteousness—everything else, including: food, drink, clothing, shelter, cars, wealth, and prosperity, will be added unto you."

—————————— ⌘ ——————————

When people are in constant need of material things,
it is evident they are not seeking the Kingdom of God
and its righteousness.

—————————— ⌘ ——————————

If we spend more time seeking the fulfillment of life's pleasures or its everyday needs with little or no time dedicated to seeking the Kingdom of God and its righteousness, then the Kingdom is not a priority in our lives, as Jesus said it should be.

"33But seek first the Kingdom of God and His righteousness, and all these things shall be added to you." Matthew 6.33

Remember, this verse contains the essence of the message He was purposed to preach on Earth: the Kingdom of God and its righteousness. Later, He ended the sermon by presenting the keys to which we can live worry-free. He taught that by placing the Kingdom in a place of priority in our lives, all other things—the things we need or long for—will be added. Praise God!

Are we ready to make the Kingdom of God and its righteousness a priority in our lives? Are we encouraged to seek the Kingdom, diligently? Are we passionate about experiencing the manifestation of the supernatural government of God: the miracles, healing, deliverance, and salvation it brings? Are we finally ready to earnestly seek the Kingdom and become instruments in the hands of God to extend it throughout the land?

If our answer is, "Yes!" to all the questions, than we need to declare the following prayer out loud, right now. Please pray with me: "Lord, here I am, send me. I want to take your justice and righteousness to those who are hurting. I want to unite with those who long to see the inherent rights of the Kingdom prevail, and I want to do works of social justice. Use me, Lord. I will go!"

Accepting the challenge
of carrying out the Kingdom's justice
creates an eternal reward.

Chapter 4

Three Absolutes: Jesus, the Kingdom, and His Word

We live in a world where absolute irrefutable truth is non-existent. Today, our society has lost the knowledge of what is true and no longer considers it a moral value or essential for life. Academic institutions teach that truth is relative, temporary, and subject to change. Consequently, we live in a society that lacks moral values and where our children no longer have absolute truths on which to build their lives. Shockingly, some cultures speak languages in which the words *truth* or *forgive* do not exist, but they do have an abundance of words to express *vengeance;* for instance, Africa and India.

Contrary to those countries, the language spoken by western society does include the word *truth*. Unfortunately, it is rarely used. This is tragic because to rarely use the word *truth* is worse than not having it—in the absence of truth there is great confusion. In our culture, the word *truth* has lost its original meaning.

Ignoring the positive influence truth can cause and overlooking the negative consequences for disregarding it, affects our present generation, and it will continue to do so at a greater degree in future generations. Why? Because future generations will grow and exist on a foundation not built on genuine strong moral values. According to the situation at hand, life and everything we know will become relative and subject to modification. The reason this chapter was written was to establish three absolute universal truths that exist and which complement each other without contradiction: Jesus, the Kingdom of God, and the Word of God.

❖ **Jesus:** He is the King of the divine government. The absolute person, absolute truth, absolute way, and the absolute and unchanging life. He is the only Savior—the only Mediator between God the Father and mankind and the only One who lived on Earth as one hundred percent man and one hundred percent God.

"⁸Jesus Christ is the same yesterday, today, and forever." Hebrews 13.8

❖ **The Kingdom of God:** This is the absolute order, absolute government, absolute authority, and absolute *will* of its King. It is the unshakeable Kingdom.

"²⁸Therefore, since we are receiving a Kingdom which cannot be shaken, let us have grace, by which we may serve God acceptably with reverence and godly fear." Hebrews 12.28

❖ **The Word of God:** It is infallible, absolute, eternal, and inspired by God; it is the written constitution of the Kingdom.

"¹⁶All Scripture is given by inspiration of God, and is profitable for doctrine, for reproof, for correction, for instruction in righteousness..." 2 Timothy 3.16

These absolute truths come together as one—one cannot exist without the other. Throughout Scripture, especially in the New Testament, we see these words used, interchangeably, but always with the same significance.

"²³So when they had appointed him a day, many came to him at his lodging, to whom he explained and solemnly testified of the Kingdom of God, persuading them concerning Jesus from both the Law of Moses and the Prophets, from morning till evening." Acts 28.23

Accepting Jesus as Lord and Savior leads to heaven.
However, failure to discover His Kingdom,
will keep us from enjoing what we have.

The discovery and acceptance of Jesus as Lord and Savior of our lives implies having a one way ticket directly to heaven. However, if we fail to discover His Kingdom, our one way ticket will not be to heaven. Moreover, our life on Earth will be unbearable. Receiving the revelation of the King, the Kingdom, and the Word is important because a king without a kingdom is only a figure head without authority. Likewise, a kingdom without a king also lacks authority. Jesus is the One, the only role model capable of representing both king and kingdom, in addition to teaching us the three absolutes. Why? Because He is the incarnate Word of God who dwells among His people.

Why did Jesus come on Earth?

"⁴³...but He said to them, "I must preach the Kingdom of God to the other cities also, because for this purpose I have been sent." Luke 4.43

Jesus was clear about His mission. He declared it, confirmed it, and carried it out, as seen in Luke 4.43. His ministry took off by preaching the Kingdom. Furthermore, for the next three and a half years leading to His death, and for forty days after his resurrection (until His ascension to Heaven), He continued to preach on the same subject: the Kingdom of God. His passion and endless teachings on the Kingdom demonstrate how important it is to Him.

"³...to whom He also presented Himself alive after His suffering by many infallible proofs, being seen by them during forty days and speaking of the things pertaining to the kingdom of God." Acts 1.3

Throughout His ministry, Jesus invested a great amount of time teaching and equipping His disciples. He taught them by illustrating, modeling, and manifesting the Kingdom. He was the only One who could do this because He was one hundred percent God and one hundred percent man. He understood what it meant to be human and God at the same time.

Why has society lost its moral values?

Western society has been under attack by four demonic spirits (these will be mentioned in detail later in the chapter) whose only purpose is to destroy the Biblical fundamentals that sustain our society; for that reason, the truth has become less than popular.

We know that Jesus—the King—is the absolute and undeniable truth; that the Kingdom of God is the absolute order and authority and the inspired word of God; and, that it contains the norms of the Kingdom as its formal constitution. Let us focus now on the study of the truth since this area has been heavily attacked.

What is the truth?

Truth is the highest level of reality that exists in heaven, on Earth, and under the Earth; it never changes—it is eternally unchanged.

The word for *truth*, in Greek, is the word *emeth*; it means: firmness, faithfulness, truth, sureness, reliability, stability, continuance, faithfulness, and credibility.

"[37]...for this cause I was born, and for this cause I have come into the world, that I should bear witness to the truth. Everyone who is of the truth hears My voice." [38]*Pilate said to Him, "What is truth?"*
John 18.37, 38

Pilate had no idea what truth was, and even when it stood before him, personified as Jesus, he failed to recognize it.

There are four demonic spirits set to destroy the truth in those who are simple-minded. Most Christian-Judean people maintain this way of thinking. Regrettably, it paves the way for the devil's constant warpath—throughout the centuries, the devil has sought to destroy those who choose Christ as King and Lord of their lives.

What is simple-minded thinking?

Simpleminded thinking is based on the declaration of a thesis and antithesis. It is a line of thought which equates or is parallel to "black and white thinking" and "gray areas."

What is a thesis?

A thesis is a theory, notion, opinion, point of view, consideration, principle, or judgment. It is a proposal that must be approved through argumentation; a written project that students prepare and submit as a final requisite, prior to graduation, in which they try to prove their point of view, idea, hypothesis, or proposal.

What is an antithesis?

An antithesis is the direct opposite of a thesis; an opposition, obstacle, or impediment that is presented as a parallel order of truths which are not necessarily negative; in other words, two truths that run parallel to each other but in the opposite direction. A thesis and antithesis can be totally opposite, like a truth and a lie.

What is biblical thesis and antithesis?

Biblical thesis and antithesis are based on the firm belief that there is only one unique and absolute truth. Once the truth is chosen, everything contrary to it becomes a lie. There is only one truth, not half-truths or conditional truths—truth is truth. The Bible consists of absolute truths: good and bad, right and wrong—truth comes from God and lies come from Satan.

Jesus, His Kingdom, and His Word are absolute truths.
Anything contrary to them is a fallacy.

The Bible is a book full of black and white truths. It establishes there is a heaven and hell; truth and lies; God and the devil; good and evil, and much more. For instance, if the Bible declares that Jesus is our only Savior, then the matter is settled. There is no other savior! Salvation, good deeds, or religion cannot come from Satan. Why? Because there is one absolute truth and that is: There is only one true God; making all other gods false. There is another absolute truth: No one comes to the Father except through Jesus Christ. This truth establishes that all other existing gods in the world, like Buddha and Allah, cannot be the absolute truth because, Jesus, alone, is the absolute truth.

"⁵Thomas said to Him, "Lord, we do not know where You are going, and how can we know the way?" ⁶Jesus said to him, "I am the way, the truth, and the life. No one comes to the Father except through Me." John 14.5, 6

What is *synthetic thinking*?

Modern pagan society introduced another mentality known as *synthetic thinking*. This mindset accepts half truths, exchanging truths for lies, and all types of theories, religions, and philosophies, including human concupiscence and lifestyles independent from God's government.

Synthetic thinking argues that each sincere point of view has something good to offer. It forces people who "want the truth" to consider every point of view without prejudice. They must accept those views as truth, yet not as the absolute truth because, in time, they might receive yet another "truth" they are currently unaware of. Due to its temporary, relative, and "subject to change" nature, this mentality is incapable of producing an absolute truth. Accordingly, gray areas are permitted and are rather extensive.

What is the end result of this synthetic mentality?

As previously stated, in synthetic thinking, there is no such thing as permanent truth. The absence of absolute truth causes people to endlessly search for it, without ever finding. Therefore, they are never satiated. Its end result is failure, due to their inability to build a firm foundation for their lives causing their existence to be unstable and constantly subject to change.

However, with biblical thesis and antithesis, there is an absolute truth—a truth that never changes. The Kingdom of God is an absolute truth and the highest level of reality we could ever discover. In today's society, the truth about moral values, family, and God is lost. The absence of absolute truth has caused the younger generation to live without limitations when practicing acts of immorality. "If what we consider to be true today can change tomorrow, then why hold on to that temporary truth?" This statement reflects the mindset that endorses young people to live in total absence of moral values and fundamentals. To them, truth is always relative, negotiable, and changeable; to them, truth is neither permanent nor absolute.

When the majority lives according to synthetic thinking, with no values or reasons for which to live or die, we are inevitably left with a shortage of genuinely committed leaders. Men become leaders out of convenience; many politicians are selfish and void of values seeking only power and wealth. They place the Word of God in the same level as partial and questionable credibility—more so than any other group of supposed truths. They wonder if what they hear is the final truth or if another truth is going to suddenly come to life. They fail to fully commit because they are afraid of becoming loyal supporters of something they question to be real.

On the one hand, radical Muslims are capable of dying for what they believe; their thinking is black and white. They are blinded by the antithesis of the absolute truth. They take something totally opposed to the Word of God and accept it as truth. They take explosives and strap them to their bodies, in a suicidal act, and kill thousands of innocent people because they are convinced that is the only way out for their people. They are willing to give up their lives for a lie that they blindly believe in and which they consider to be an absolute truth. On the other hand, Westerners are incapable of dying for their faith because that faith is subject to constant changes. Sadly, radical Muslims are willing to die for a lie while Christians cannot even *live* for the absolute truth!

If we fail to radically believe in God's truth, we will never *willingly* give up our lives for it.

How did this change take place in the human mind?

At the end of the twentieth century, Christians and Jews were influenced by German and Greek philosophers who introduced a new way of thinking to the educational system in Western countries. The numerous schools founded by the Greeks experienced an increase in philosophical teachings, which were quickly spread worldwide through their (Greek and Roman) victories. The Romans conquered and used their victories to expand the Greek mentality which was "in style" at the time. As a result, we also inherited their mentality; it quickly affected our science, psychology, anthropology, astronomy, and every discipline that involved humanity.

Today, when you attend any university in Europe, the United States, or Latin America it is easy to recognize that the *black and white mentality* does not exist. Those who feed on that mentality are considered strange for believing in only one truth and are often bombarded with the suggestions to consider other truths, to not be close-minded, to keep on open mind, etc. They consider Christians ignorant and oldfashioned because, unlike Christians, they accept the fanfare of transitory truths taught by philosophies throughout classrooms and churches. Now, let us learn which four spirits and/or mentalities were brought to our shores by these philosophies:

❖ **The spirit of Greece: Humanism and Intellectualism**

Most of us were trained to think synthetically by the spirit of Greece that infiltrated our universities, colleges, and churches, but the worst part is that we allowed it. This does not imply that we should keep our children from attending the university or seeking a higher level of education. Of course we will send them! However, before we let them go into the world of humanism and intellectualism, we must teach them, at home and at church, to think *black and white*. This way, when they are confronted with adulthood, synthetic thinking will not lead them astray. We must diligently help our children gain wisdom and maturity in the area of spiritual discernment so they can learn to distinguish between world philosophies and biblical truths and choose wisely.

The first attack is the devil's deliberate assault to confuse us— mentally—and to keep us from distinguishing good from evil. Greek mentality is a curse! Society demands that Christians be tolerant and accepting of the lies that deny the existence of God as if it were an absolute truth, what is worse is that we idly stand by, doing nothing to stop it! Someone has to stand up in defense of the truth even if that moment of courage results in the loss of position and persecution. We must defend the absolute truths of the Kingdom of God because they are the only solid foundation society has.

How did the devil attack our society with that mentality? Our society was attacked by the spirit of Greece through the educational system and the media. Once that synthetic mentality penetrated the minds of professionals and the people in general, the second attack came:

❖ **The spirit of the anti-Christ:** This (spirit) challenges and questions the Bible's veracity by asking a controversial question, "Who can prove the Bible is true?"

After our society was attacked by this synthetic mentality, Scripture started being questioned. So much so, that the seed was left planted in the minds and hearts of people and growing throughout the generations. That seed of doubt grew and bore fruit resulting in a mentality that believes the Bible is *not* the absolute truth; this, is the spirit of anti-Christ. The combination of abandoning Biblical doctrine along with Satan's relentless dissatisfaction (the destructive results were not enough), resulted in a third attack:

The spirit of antichrist
challenges and questions the veracity of the Bible, in order
to cause confusion and destroy our faith in Christ.

❖ **Sexual immorality**

A society not founded on the Word of God is destined for failure. Without its fundamental parameters for life, such as the family, marriage covenant (between one man and one woman), and respect towards parents, society is bound to suffer the dangers, and the unstable fruits of the unruly lifestyle. Accordingly, the lack of moral values (based on the absolute truth), caused mankind to further surrender to the desires of their flesh. They have nothing to keep them from carrying out their fleshly desires and sinning against God; especially since the concept of sin, according to the synthetic mentality, is a relative truth: one that is contingent upon the individual's point of view.

❖ **Greed and avariciousness**

People work hard to increase their wealth and provide a better quality of life for their families; they put so much time and effort into increasing their financial portfolio that, at times, they end up consumed by greed and avariciousness. Others simply want more material wealth because they believe their future security is based on having more. Unfortunately, they do it without realizing that this mentality has turned money into their god, which in turn, opens doors to the spirit of greed. The desire to become rich at any price develops the compulsive desire for material things. Suddenly, the "American dream" takes the place that belongs to God and we end up with busier lives, looking for money and provisions instead of seeking the provider of all things.

We need to seek the provider, not the provisions. Having said that, I am not endorsing a lifestyle of poverty because God's will is not for us to live in poverty. No! God wants us to prosper financially, but collecting wealth cannot be the priority in our lives.

Ministers and preachers shy away from revealing this truth for fear of criticism, being harshly attacked, persecuted, and in the worse of cases, misinterpreted or misunderstood. We live in a society that consumes different opinions that demand tolerance, freedom of speech, and opinion, but it fails to have moral values on which we can stand firm or be rooted in. Ministers of the gospel, believers, and leaders with Biblical values *cannot* negotiate the fact that Jesus, His Kingdom, and His Word are the only truth, the way to heaven, and eternal life. We must preach that the most precious treasure to be found by man is the Kingdom of God—but before doing this, the Kingdom should be a reality in our lives and we should partake of it.

These days, it is becoming commonplace, to see the theological, ideological, spiritual, and natural areas of our existence experience a powerful shakedown. Stop for a moment and answer the following questions: "How many times has the Earth trembled in the last decade? How many earthquakes, hurricanes, and tsunamis has Earth experienced in the past ten years? These events used to be rare occurrences that took place few and far between—the operative words being *used to be*. History tells the story of many changes taking place which are changing and shaping the direction of mankind. During the eighties, the foundation and strength of communism was shaken. After 9/11 and the tsunami, the same happened to capitalism, socialism, the stock market, and the world's economy. In the area of health, the foundation was also shaken with the increase in the number of individuals reported to be suffering with AIDS, cancer, leukemia, hepatitis, and more.

When the doctor shakes his head and says you have cancer, the news shakes you down to the core of your being. When an unmarried daughter tells you she is pregnant, when a child runs away from home, when the business is on the verge of bankruptcy, when your marriage is about to end in divorce, your life suffers a serious shakedown. Yet, as these things take place around you, three things remain the same—unshaken and unchanging: Jesus, His Word, and His Kingdom. Therefore, we must understand, accept, and believe these three absolutes because when the foundation of our lives is shaken, these three will be the anchor that will see us through it all.

How can we be free from the influence of the spirit of Greece, the spirit of the anti-Christ, immorality, and greed?

To be free from these spirits, we must:

❖ **Believe in the three absolute truths: Jesus, His Word, and His Kingdom**

In a changing world, where everything is in constant movement, people need a firm foundation that can stabilize their lives, but for this to take place, they must know there is only one person who never changes: Jesus. There is only one unshakeable Kingdom: the Kingdom of God. Only one true and eternal word: the Word of God. You can come to Jesus today or tomorrow, and He will always be the same loving, compassionate, righteous, and forgiving King who is always able to guarantee security, courage, and strength for your life. Jesus is the Savior. He is the same yesterday and today, and we know this because He healed yesterday and continues to heal today. He delivered the captives free, yesterday, and continues to deliver, today. He is the unchanging strength people are struggling to find today, but it can only be found in Jesus, His Kingdom, and His Word.

"8Jesus Christ (the Messiah) is [always] the same, yesterday, today, [yes] and forever (to the ages)."Hebrews 13.8—AMP

Throughout the ages, revolts have risen against Jesus, His Kingdom, and the Word, but these have remained intact and unchanging because they are unshakeable. These three basic truths make it possible for men to achieve complete satisfaction and provision that can never be found in any religion—these truths make men free and pave the way for everyone to enjoy a fulfilled life.

The Kingdom of God is unshakeable;
nothing can destroy it. However, disobedience
displaces it and gives way for the kingdom of darkness.

"28Let us therefore, receiving a Kingdom that is firm and stable and cannot be shaken, offer to God pleasing service and acceptable worship, with modesty and pious care and godly fear and awe."
Hebrews 12.28—AMP

❖ **Believe that Jesus is the only mediator between God and men.**

"⁵For there [is only] one God, and [only] one Mediator between God and men, the Man Christ Jesus..." 1 Timothy 2.5

If there is only one God, then all others are false. There is only one mediator who takes the hand of both, God the Father and man, and joins them to restore peace between the two. Jesus is the only One in whom we find salvation.

"¹²Nor is there salvation in any other, for there is no other name under heaven given among men by which we must be saved."
Acts 4.12

The Greek word for *other* is the word *heteros*, which means: another; one not of the same nature, form, class, or kind—generic distinction; it also means distinction and exclusivity without other alternatives, opinions, or options. Jesus is the only One; there is no other. The Kingdom, the Word, and Jesus are absolute truths, everything else is a lie, and we must be courageous enough to proclaim it!

The Kingdom, the Word, and the Kingdom: reality or idealism?

A thesis is tested by argumentation with proof that the proposition is true. The definition of truth is: the highest level of reality, stability, and security that exists.

How do we prove the thesis that affirms Jesus, His Word, and His Kingdom as the absolute truth? Before going into it, I want to establish that I am a realist, not an idealist. A realist is one that sees things as they really are, without underestimating the situation at hand and without exaggeration. My standpoint is one hundred percent realist. Therefore, nothing of that I will explain comes from my imagination or the simple desire to believe in *something* without discovering the veracity of the Kingdom, the Word, and the person of Jesus. Having established this, let us proceed to prove this thesis with the following truths:

❖ The Word became flesh

"14And the Word became flesh and dwelt among us, and we beheld His glory, the glory as of the only begotten of the Father, full of grace and truth." John 1.14

In every other religion, the word is just a word, but for us, the Word was Jesus, and the Word became flesh to dwell in us. In essence, the *ideal* came and made Himself *real*—the invisible became visible. Everything Jesus taught He modeled in His human form. He was everything His words declared He was. His works and words are interchangeable because they always complement each other and go together. The Word became flesh in the person of Jesus—He was what His words said He was.

"19And He said to them, "What things?" So they said to Him, "The things concerning Jesus of Nazareth, who was a Prophet mighty in deed and word before God and all the people..." Luke 24.19

When Jesus finished the sermon, some considered Him to be an idealist while others said He spoke with authority, but He was more than that. All of reality was *in* Him. Jesus was not a moralist. His purpose was not to merely impose a moral code; rather, Jesus, is the One who revealed *what is real*—truth is the highest level of reality that exists in heaven and on Earth. The truth of God operates in the visible and invisible world.

Truth is the highest level of reality
that exists in heaven and Earth.

Some religions believe they know what is right for mankind, but they try to accomplish it in their human strength. On the other hand, those who are part of the Kingdom do not *try* to be better or happier because we simply *are;* God gives us the power to be happy when His word becomes "flesh"—real—in our lives. Consequently, we are no longer struggling to find happiness, we just *are* happy. Religion tries to make people better human beings, but Jesus and His Kingdom make people different through regeneration! When Christ—the Verb—enters the heart of an individual, He becomes flesh in that person and regenerates his whole being; this causes a total transformation in the person.

We know the Word became flesh when a drug addict no longer craves the drug; when it heals the sick or when it delivers an alcoholic. In short, the Word becomes flesh when what it says becomes something tangible. In our ministry, we can testify of the hundreds of people who received salvation, were healed, delivered, and transformed. We see how God prospers them because they choose to believe in the three absolute truths. The Word becomes flesh—real and tangible in their lives. Their faces change; their attitudes change; and their lives are transformed.

Let us read a few testimonies of real people whose lives were transformed by Jesus:

Testimony of Dr. Joaquín Tomás

My grandparents were born in Spain, and I am the son of Cuban immigrants. I came to the United States to experience the American dream. I thought I could be happy if only I had enough money, social recognition, respect, and academic excellence. My ambition made me successful. I completed my Doctorate in Medicine and became a surgeon. I was awarded a Fellowship in Oncology surgery and received a Masters in Surgical Pathology. With these degrees, I had recognition, social and academic respect, wealth, and held an honorable position in the community. I was successful in my public life, but my personal life was a total disaster. I was divorced several times, and my personal moral values were quickly deteriorating due to corrupt behavior and the abuse of several toxic substances. I was unhappy, depressed, and constantly contemplated suicide. There was something missing in my apparently successful life and accomplishments. That something was fundamental for my survival.

One day, I was invited to a church to hear some famous singers, but the only reason I went was to hear the music and enjoy the artists. There, through the worship music, the Lord touched my heart, and I was able to recognize how lost I really was. The spiritual blindness I had for so long was gone, and I was finally able to recognize that what was truly missing in my life was Jesus!

I am still ambitious, only not for worldly things but for the Kingdom of God. My life finally makes sense and has purpose. I have peace in my heart; I know where I am going; and I am certain of my destiny. Jesus became flesh *in* me and gave me a new life.

Testimony of Marianne Salazar

On July 2005, my seventy-three year old mother was in the hospital. According to her doctors, she was in the final stages of Hepatitis C, had cirrhosis of the liver, and desperately needed a liver donor if she were to survive. The doctors only gave her weeks to live. We were desperate and running out of time.

I am a lawyer. I enjoyed excellent health, was successful in my profession, had great friends, and had everything a person could need or want; everything seemed perfect, except for the fact that my mother was dying. On Sunday, July 17, 2005, my mother saw Pastor Maldonado's program on television and asked me to take her to one of the healing crusades he had talked about on the program. I did. When the pastor called forward everyone who had been diagnosed with blood disorders, specifically Hepatitis C, I did not have to be asked twice. I took my mother to the altar where the pastor prayed for her. Since that moment, her health has been gradually improving. Her liver regenerated and started to clean her body of toxins without the need for a transplant. The doctors were in shock; they ran every scientific test known to man, until finally, they had to recognize that a miracle of God had taken place in her body. The Word became flesh in her.

Today, I am a Christian woman. After all, who can argue against a miracle? My life changed completely. I enjoy a wonderful relationship with God, through His Son, Jesus, and it is more intimate and precious than ever. I am totally convinced He has a purpose for me in His Kingdom and am ready to carry it out through a covenant relationship with Him—all that I do is for His glory!

Testimony of Juan Guzmán

For twenty years, I was a baseball player in the major leagues. I participated in two world series and won two rings in recognition for my achievements (receiving these rings is the dream of every athlete). I was counted among the top ten best pitchers. I was a guest player in an All-Star game. I met famous, wealthy, and influential people. I signed several multimillion dollar contracts, purchased all types of real estate, and invested much of my earnings. I guess you could say I had fame, wealth, and position, as far as the world was concerned, yet with all my accomplishments, my life was empty. It was this realization that made me turn to God. When I did, I made the conscious decision to remove from my life the things I knew were displeasing to Him. I stopped having meaningless relationships with women and asked God to give me a wife, and He did! After a series of inconveniences in my country, we moved to Miami where we found El Rey Jesus church. There, we felt the presence of God like never before. We knew we had come home. I have never been the same since.

My life was transformed by the power and love of God. The emptiness and void I used to feel is now full of His presence. I have a family, and I lead an ordered and disciplined life. I have goals, purpose, real friends, and an exciting destiny in Christ. Jesus became flesh in my life!

Testimony of Andy Argüez

I grew up in a dysfunctional home. I saw my mother suffer under my father's abuse until I was six years old, which is when he left home. My heart was hardened. I felt lost and without identity; and so, I hit the streets hoping to discover who I was and perhaps even find my direction in life. In the streets, I sold drugs and was a gang member. I was handy with a gun and learned how to escape the police and the bullets that constantly grazed my head. I was a young man looking for someone to love me and give me a sense of who I was—I needed identity. I missed not hearing my father say, "I love you!"

One morning, before dawn, I was on the streets selling drugs with my buddies when another gang approached us, pointed their guns at our heads, and started to shoot. While the bullets looked for their victims, the police helicopters flew overhead. It was at that instant that I cried out to God to spare and save my life. I completely surrendered to Him, and His power changed my heart. That day, fifteen years later, I was able to cry again and finally forgive my father. Today, I live to worship my God and to rescue the young people who are living under the same circumstances that I did because I want them to receive the love of the Father and for His Word to become flesh in them, as it did in me.

❖ **A testimony is unquestionable proof**

"[11] And they overcame him by the blood of the Lamb and by the word of their testimony, and they did not love their lives to the death." Revelation 12.11

The testimony of an individual who is transformed by the power of God is something no one can argue against. *The person with an argument will always be at the mercy of the one with a lived experience.* John tells us that the devil is defeated by the power of the blood and the testimony of what Jesus did in our lives from the moment we entered His Kingdom.

Christianity, then, is not an illusion or idealism; it is a truth that manifests itself and becomes "flesh," the same way Jesus, the King, became flesh. He died and was raised so that His life could become the embodied truth in us. The Kingdom of God, Jesus, and the Word of God are three absolute truths that are steadfast, constant, and changeless. On them lies the seal of approval and validation Jesus placed when He was raised from the dead.

———————

A person with an argument will always lose to the one who has experience.

———————

Chapter 5

FUNDAMENTAL
PRINCIPLES
OF THE KINGDOM

The fundamental principles of the Kingdom are found in the Beatitudes, taught by Jesus in the beginning of His ministry, when He preached the Sermon on the Mount. Due to the fullness of its content, it is one of the most comprehensive teachings we can find. It is based on the principles that rule the Kingdom of God, in such a way, that it establishes the righteousness of the Kingdom, on Earth, and the will of its King.

Interestingly enough, we learn that before Jesus delivered this message, He prepared the hearts and minds of the people, compelling them to change their mentality. He did this in view of the powerful principles He was about to teach them because they needed their minds to be open and willing to receive the news of the Kingdom.

"¹⁷From that time Jesus began to preach and to say, "Repent, for the Kingdom of heaven is at hand." Matthew 4.17

The word **repent** implies that we have a complete change of mind in order to change our lifestyle. Jesus challenged the multitude to leave behind the old paradigms and mental schemes that kept them from entering the Kingdom. My dear reader, you are also being given this challenge today so you can open your mind and be able to understand these powerful principles. If you allow this to take place, your life will never again be the same.

I once had the opportunity to visit Israel and stand where Jesus delivered the Sermon on the Mount. The sensation was extraordinary! I was able to imagine Jesus teaching, under the anointing of the Holy Spirit, to thousands of people who crowded around to hear Him. The message and the challenge are as strong today as they were then because it continues to touch and transform lives.

It is important to note that the two most important teachings Jesus gave were the *Sermon at the Mount* and *The Lord's Prayer*. In both, He mentioned the Kingdom of God; this confirms, once more, that the Kingdom was a priority for Jesus. Before we dive into this very passionate subject, let us, first, discuss the circumstances under which Jesus taught the *Sermon at the Mount*.

What is the *Sermon at the Mount?*

The name derives from the fact the sermon was preached on the Mount. A multitude and the disciples of Jesus gathered together to listen to the Master. *The Sermon at the Mount* is not so much a teaching urging the people to hear the principles of the Kingdom, but rather, it was a way to exhibit or illustrate Jesus' life and of those who had entered the Kingdom.

Many consider the *Sermon on the Mount* to be a type of utopia; idealism impossible to practice in everyday life. However, Jesus taught it as something that was real and possible; something every believer could manifest and live on Earth, with the help and guidance of the Holy Spirit.

The Sermon on the Mount is a group or set of fundamental principles, attitudes, and ways of thinking that are exposed, not imposed, so they can be lived and experienced. It is the character of King Jesus—the wisest and holiest being to have ever existed. These principles were given to be obeyed and practiced within the Kingdom, on Earth. This was the first teaching that produced the greatest impact and the one that Jesus used to establish the apostolic foundation and values of the Kingdom.

It is worth mentioning that during this sermon, Jesus did not mention rebuking demons or spiritual warfare. Today, many people practice spiritual warfare, bind, and loosen, before ever establishing the Kingdom. Before we enter into spiritual warfare, it is imperative that we be have a properly established foundation.

Before practicing spiritual warfare, we must make certain that our foundation is rightly planted.

How did Jesus begin the *Sermon on the Mount*?

❖ Jesus sat down

"¹And seeing the multitudes, He went up on a mountain, and when He was seated His disciples came to Him." Matthew 5.1

The *New International Version* of the Bible writes this verse in the following way:

"¹Now when He saw the crowds, He went up on a mountainside and sat down. His disciples came to Him..." Matthew 5.1

The expression *sat down* means to settle and get comfortable on the throne, with a certainty and sense of belonging; as if one has every right to occupy it. When a person sits on a throne it is because he intends to exercise the government and authority of the Kingdom from that place. In other words, to sit for the purpose of teaching means to take the seat of authority and begin to govern.

Jesus taught with His attitude. Sitting down to speak to the multitude and His disciples, in the spiritual realm meant that He was taking the throne to instruct or teach with authority—as God's representative and as God Himself. Today, we must do the same; we must teach with authority because we are ambassadors sent by the King. We are not like the Pharisees, religious, or legalist who are without authority as a consequence for living a dead law.

Through our faith in Jesus and His redeeming grace, we are the Word made flesh.

❖ Blessed

The second word Jesus teaches is **blessed.** This is the Greek word *makarios,* and it means: extremely blessed, fortunate, happy, glorious, joyful to be sent, and spiritually prosperous; with life, joy, peace, and satisfaction in the favor of God, regardless of external circumstances.

This word points to someone who has lived long and who is completely content and satisfied; this is a permanent condition in a believer—one that is established through *being,* not doing.

When Jesus spoke that word, He declared the following: Now, we are happy. We no longer have to wait to be blessed because we are already blessed, satisfied, and prosperous. He did not say "Now, do this or that to obtain it." He said for us to be what we already are. He did not say, "have" because it is not something we have to make an effort to have because we already *are* blessed. When we review the beatitudes described by Jesus, we must make an inventory of our lives to see if we are being and living what He says we are.

Two very important points:

- He sat down to teach. He took the authority to govern, from His throne, and He simply declared and established all the principles, fundamentals, values, mentalities, and attitudes of the Kingdom of God.

- He declared us blessed. Everything He said from that moment on is what we should be as a result of being blessed; therefore, moving from mere idealism to a reality. The beatitudes enclose a divine virtue that should be learned and developed.

How was the *Sermon at the Mount* presented?

Jesus presents the nine beatitudes in groups of three; this alone is enough to send us the message that no virtue works alone but in combination with others in order to bring manifestation of the Kingdom's perfect righteousness. Jesus presented the beatitudes in the following order: The first and second beatitude of each group are truths that run parallel but opposite; this is what we call "thesis and antithesis," resulting in a "synthesis." Their purpose is to create a balance in a person's character. Specifically, the third beatitude is the sum of the first two, meanwhile each virtue merits its own reward; as a result, the person is able to, simultaneously, produce wonderful results in their character.

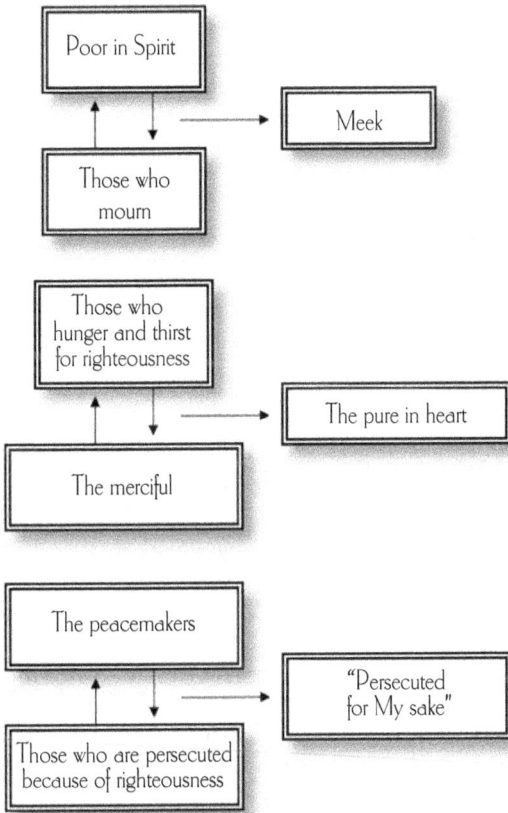

Now, let us study the fundamental principles of the Kingdom that produce long life on Earth and success in our business, relationships, politics, and/or government amongst others: The nine beatitudes. Embracing each beatitude successfully will allow us to establish a strong society, rooted in Biblical values. Why? Because they hit the key points necessary for the building of strong families, obedient children, prosperity, and having fulfilled lives.

The first group of beatitudes

1. Blessed are the poor in spirit

> *"³Blessed are the poor in spirit, for theirs is the Kingdom of heaven."* Matthew 5.3

Who are the poor in spirit?

This type of person recognizes that if he is not totally dependent on God, he will suffer spiritual bankruptcy; they are also humble and recognize they *need* God. They are teachable, mentally docile, dependent, and easily shaped; someone who knows that without God, they cannot live.

I must clarify that the poor in spirit is not someone who suffers with low self-esteem, who has a poor self-image, or whose spirit is anemic and weak; but rather, it is someone who *depends* on God.

This first principle of the Kingdom was taught because *independence* from God was the exact cause of Adam's fall. Therefore, Jesus taught this principle to break man's sinful tendencies; using it to penetrate their ego, flesh, and self-sufficiency.

> *"¹⁵For thus says the High and Lofty One who inhabits eternity, whose name is Holy: 'I dwell in the high and holy place, with him who has a contrite and humble spirit, to revive the spirit of the humble, and to revive the heart of the contrite ones.'"* Isaiah 57.15

It is those who are poor in spirit and heartbroken due to suffering and hard times that feel the need for God. Usually, their hearts are broken due to abuse; they were mistreated by society, either by unforgiveness, and or social injustice. They know they need the Lord everyday and recognize they are weak; they depend on Him, knowing they are incapable of making it without Him.

What is the reward for those who are poor in spirit?

Jesus teaches the following: "be sufficiently poor so as to receive everything that is at your disposal." If you learn to depend on God and not your own abilities, the Kingdom of God and its resources—justice, peace, joy, forgiveness, healing, power, and authority—will be yours."

Everything in the Kingdom
belongs to those who are sufficiently poor in spirit
so as to welcome those who totally depend on God.

Everything the Kingdom has belongs to those who are sufficiently poor to receive it; those who depend solely on God. This is a universal principle that can be applied to the entire human race. Man separated himself from God and became independent from Him—a decision that cost him his life; however, those who choose to live dependent on God, like Jesus did, gain eternal life and every resource of its supernatural government.

Illustration: A nursing child is sufficiently poor so as to receive his mother's milk. Otherwise, he dies of malnutrition. The baby drinks the milk because he is hungry. In other words, he depends on it. When the milk is unavailable, he cries out for it with all his strength. The man who lives independent from God feels depressed, lonely, and sick; this is referred to as spiritual death—it is impossible to live a happy life on Earth, without God.

To be hungry for God or to declare spiritual bankruptcy is just the beginning to receiving all the blessings of the Kingdom. We must always declare that there is nothing we can do in our own strength: "Without God we can do nothing!" There is no power within us that can make us successful; the power to succeed can only come from God. Jesus said the following:

"⁵I am the vine, you are the branches. He who abides in Me, and I in him, bears much fruit; for without Me you can do nothing."
John 15.5

Everything that is most valuable within the Kingdom—the greatest details of His wisdom and understanding, the most essential, the most complete information, the greatest most divine mysteries, the revelation of wisdom, and the fear of the Lord—is available to everyone who thirsts and hungers to receive it; for those who declared themselves spiritual bankrupt and desire to live dependent on Him. In other words, the mysteries are not available to those who are "better" or worthy to receive them, nor for great intellectuals, or the most talented; rather, the mysteries of the Kingdom are available and at the disposal of those who are hungry for them and are willing to receive them.

Allow me to ask you a few questions: "Are you spiritually bankrupt?" "Are you thirsty and hungry enough to receive the Kingdom?" "Do you rely on God or on your ego?"

The best of the Kingdom and its resources is available for the smallest, the sufficiently humble or poor in spirit, and for those in need and ready to receive; they are the brokenhearted who recognize they cannot live without God and who desperately cry out, longing to be filled with the Holy Spirit, the nourishment of His Word, and the fullness of His presence.

Illustration: Jesus did not trust in Himself. He was totally dependent on the Father and the Holy Spirit.

"¹⁹Then Jesus answered and said to them, "Most assuredly, I say to you, the Son can do nothing of Himself, but what He sees the Father do; for whatever He does, the Son also does in like manner." John 5.19

The Kingdom of God is for anyone, anywhere, willing to surrender to the same terms. The Kingdom has come; it has come to you—it is in you! The Kingdom is always at hand, but only those who are humble and poor in spirit receive it.

We do not have to "work" to *win* the Kingdom because it cannot be won. Although, this does not imply it was cheap to obtain, the

Kingdom is free. We receive it by *grace*. Jesus paid the price at the cross with His blood, in order for us to enjoy it. We must accept it for what it is: sovereign and absolute. His Kingdom indites Jesus as our only and absolute Lord and the only one we choose to obey, absolutely. We surrender to His will so we can live blessed and in absolute freedom.

Being "poor in spirit" is the essential beatitude for a believer to transform from one who gets "filled with happiness," to one who (as Jesus declared) *is* happy.

2. Blessed are those who mourn

"⁴Blessed are those who mourn, for they shall be comforted."
Matthew 5.4

Thesis: The second beatitude drastically contrasts the first. In the first, Jesus gives us the Kingdom and makes us happy. Now, He tells us that those who cry are blessed—this constitutes the antithesis that creates the balance in character. What did Jesus intend for us to learn? Remember, we have already established that the Lord placed the beatitudes in groups of three, each with a specific function.

When a person is saved, he rejoices because he belongs to the Kingdom and is able to enjoy all its resources. In fact, Jesus taught that this joy could lead to selfishness. In other words, it can lead us to enjoying the blessings while forgetting there are still others who need to know Jesus and are yet to enter the Kingdom. To avoid this extreme, Jesus leads us to the opposite, and yet, parallel truth; thus, creating a just balance in our lives.

Who are they that mourn?

One who mourns is compassionate toward those who are lost without Christ and who have yet to enter the Kingdom. They cry for those who are afraid, anxious, and sad; for those who are enslaved to the bondage of sin, poverty, wretchedness, and ignorance. Unlike, the first stage, where they are happily enjoying the Kingdom and its righteousness, now, they *cry* for others to enter the Kingdom. This is not referring to two different people; the same person can feel happy to be in the Kingdom and at the same time cry for those who are not.

In Scripture, we find that those who cry or mourn for the needs of others are intercessors. They are compassionate and cry out, as if with labor pains, for any individual or situation in need of Christ and the Kingdom. Our cry should be against acts of injustice and for the pain and misery of those who have yet to receive the Kingdom.

Jesus said we would be blessed if we mourn for those who are depressed, alone, sick, and above all—lost. We must cry for them because the Kingdom is not about one person receiving it or enjoying it privately and selfishly; but rather, it is for everyone to receive and enjoy, collectively. It is God's desire to see *all* His children enjoying the blessings, health, peace, justice, and joy found in His Kingdom.

What is Jesus' reward to those who mourn?

People who mourn for the salvation of the lost will be comforted with a mantle of joy and gladness.

"3...to console those who mourn in Zion, to give them beauty for ashes, the oil of joy for mourning, the garment of praise for the spirit of heaviness; that they may be called trees of righteousness, the planting of the LORD, that He may be glorified" Isaiah 61.3

When we pray for someone to receive the Lord, and they do, the joy and gladness of the Kingdom becomes real in our lives.

We will never see a transformation in our children, churches, ministries, cities, or nations until we cry and mourn for them; until we begin to pour out our soul for those we want God to transform. The cry that redeems is not one that simply sheds a tear or two; it is a heavy cry—one with the burden for others to enjoy the Kingdom. First, we must ask God for this burden, so we may earnestly cry out for God to touch them with His gifts of salvation, prosperity, and righteousness.

Being anxious to see the Kingdom manifest can be a beautiful feeling, because without it, we would never be capable of crying out for people who are in desperate need. If you love your city and nation, you will cry out for them. If not, you will be indifferent towards them and that will keep you from enjoying the blessings of the Kingdom.

3. Blessed are the meek

"⁵Blessed are the meek, for they shall inherit the Earth." Matthew 5.5

Who are the meek?

The best way to define those who are meek is: those who do not worry about themselves nor are concerned how others see them. Another definition is humbleness—this is the synthesis. Meek does not mean weak or lacking in character. Biblically speaking, a meek person is someone who is detached from himself and lives passionately for God.

In accordance with genuine humility mentioned in the Bible, an individual who is genuinely meek does not worry about his reputation. Their desire is to carry out the will of God because they are consumed by their love for the Kingdom which provokes the passion to carry out God's will. In other words, real humility means to deny oneself in order to magnify the purpose of God. These are the meek or humble the Bible mentions that will inherit the Earth and everything in it.

Illustration: Moses was meek and humble.

"³Now the man Moses was very meek (gentle, kind, and humble) or above all the men on the face of the Earth." Numbers 12.3—AMP

Moses is the author of the first five books in the Bible—otherwise known as the Pentateuch (Numbers being one of those books). With Moses being the author of the above verse , we see that *he* wrote about himself in that manner; yet, the misconception of humility or meekness that most have, would not allow them to accept a "meek" person to comment on themselves as he did, because it would seem boastful. However, this verse proves that the Biblical meaning of meek is not the same as the world's. Further, the following verse shows that Jesus, also declared himself as meek and humble.

"29Take My yoke upon you and learn of Me, for I am gentle (meek) and humble (lowly) in heart, and you will find rest (relief and ease and refreshment and recreation and blessed quiet) for your souls." Matthew 11.29—AMP

Jesus and Moses did not say they were interested in themselves or looking to satisfy their personal agenda, nor were they selfish or worried about their reputations. On the contrary, they were diligently demonstrating their passion for the Kingdom. The passion of the meek and humble rests in establishing, preaching, observing, and extending, by force, the Kingdom of God on Earth. The Kingdom and the purposes of God are too great and overwhelming to waste time worrying about the "self." This is how Jesus and Moses perceived things to be. They successfully made their meekness and humility as examples worthy to be followed in order to bring the Kingdom of God on Earth.

Today, "the meek" are scarce. Most waste too much time worrying about their own reputation than that of Jesus—causing them to miss their inheritance.

What reward can the meek expect to receive?

They shall inherit the Earth. Meekness is a combination of two virtues within Jesus' character: His hunger and thirst to receive from God and His sensibility to the pain of those who suffer life crisis due to not having the Lord. Meekness brings about men and women void of all selfishness; people who, regardless of the great blessings they inherit, continue to be sensitive, humble, and dependent on God. They do not seek the Kingdom to satisfy a personal agenda because they genuinely love Jesus, His Kingdom, and His people; thus, these shall inherit the Earth!

Meekness is not a sign of weakness.
It is a virtue deriving from a strong character
that does not surrender until it sees Jesus
and His Kingdom established.

The first group of beatitudes Jesus taught refers to the poor in spirit: they are those who need God, receive the Kingdom, and are happy; they mourn for those who do not have the Kingdom of God or Jesus. When these two collide, they produce a meek individual—one who loses interest in personal gain and is passionate for God. Again, meekness does not *equate* weakness; rather it is the result of being dependent on God and sensitive enough to cry out for the masses that are living outside and may, otherwise, never enter the Kingdom.

Let us keep in mind that the first three beatitudes interrelate; one cannot go without the other. If we are poor in spirit but do not cry out for salvation to reach others, we continue to be weak. On the other hand, if we apply these two virtues, they will make us meek, strong, and ready to inherit the Earth and any other blessing of the Kingdom. The best part of embracing this is that it affects our character in a positive way. Praise God! Let us pray for the Lord to make these three virtues a part of our character so we can be blessed.

The second group of beatitudes

In the second group of beatitudes, Jesus, once more, affirms the fact that hunger, thirst, and dependence on God are the most important virtues one can have. Our hunger and thirst becomes powerful forces pushing us to live with the virtuous character of Jesus. When people live to satisfy this hunger and thirst, they lose their reputation, become irrepressible, and walk away from the principles of human protocol (such as manmade bureaucracies).

4. **Blessed are those who hunger and thirst for righteousness**

"⁶Blessed are those who hunger and thirst for righteousness, for they shall be filled." Matthew 5.6

What is righteousness?

Thesis: Righteousness is a sovereign attribute of God that allows Him to govern with impartiality and bring salvation to mankind. Righteousness means to restore and cause rights to prevail and to perform works of social justice. The righteousness of the Kingdom was sufficiently explained in chapter three. Therefore, we will only cover the part that pertains to the beatitude at hand.

"Blessed are those who hunger and thirst for righteousness..." This verse contains two key words:

- **Hunger**. *Peinao* is the Greek word for hunger, and it means: to be needy, to crave ardently, or to seek with eager desire.

- **Thirst**. *Dipsao* is the Greek word for thirst, and it means: to suffer from thirst. Figuratively speaking, it also means those who are said to thirst; who painfully feel a longing and eagerly yearn for that by which the soul is refreshed, supported, and strengthened.

According to what Jesus teaches in the beatitudes, righteousness is about the struggle to make rights prevail. Based on this, we could rephrase the verse to read: "Blessed are those who have intense hunger and who thirst to seek and do whatever is necessary to make rights prevail because they will be filled."

Jesus was talking about men and women who fight to see that everyone executes their right to receive and enjoy health, security, food, shelter, clothing, education, work, and more. The Lord is talking to individuals who, beyond wishing for, have the extreme passion, the intense hunger to make sure the rights of the poor and abused prevail; hunger to see that the younger generations execute their right to get an education; hunger to see abused and mistreated children be kindly treated and receive the love they are so desperately crying out for; thirsty to see men delivered from depression and for the lost to receive salvation. This is a piercing desire and intense thirst that refuses to be satiated until they see results (people being respected and their rights protected). Are you one who hungers and thirsts for righteousness?

What is the reward for those who hunger and thirst for righteousness?

Their hunger and thirst for righteousness will be satisfied when they witness the impoverished and abused receive what they ardently fought for them to receive. People who fight to protect the rights of others will be filled with joy, peace, salvation, prosperity, health, and much more.

5. **Blessed are the merciful**

"Blessed are the merciful, for they shall obtain mercy." Matthew 5.7

Who are the merciful?

Antithesis: Merciful is he who sympathizes with the needy—the wicked, the sinners, those who ignore the law, liars, and those who do not deserve forgiveness; he who does not demand justice according to others' evil deeds but who repays evil with good.

This is what our God did while we lived deep in our crimes and sin. He did not demand justice according to our evil deeds, but rather, He was merciful and justified us by canceling the wages of our debt and clothing us with robes of righteousness and purity. Mercy is the opposed but parallel truth that works in conjunction with righteousness.

"¹⁰Mercy and truth have met together; righteousness and peace have kissed." Psalms 85.10

Righteousness gives people
what they "deserve" (punishment); mercy does not.

Although these attributes seemingly contradict, they actually complement each other; they harmonize the righteous *and* merciful character of God in the believer. Righteousness on its own can dangerously lead people to become judgmental and intolerant toward those who behave improperly. People can become radical rights activists, to the extent that, if not careful, can develop a *creator's complex.* In other words, one who considers himself the only righteous one, the only one who is never wrong, and the only one who fights to establish the rights of others; this type of behavior and mentality can cause one to become hard, unmerciful, and irrational and cause their victories of righteousness to become bitter events best forgotten.

I know people who do not tolerate injustice. They defend what they believe to be right with all they have, but in their efforts to achieve justice, they become hard and unyielding with sinners and those who ignore the truth. They forget that mercy is as much a virtue of God as justice and that *both* must be exercised before establishing any sense of right and wrong. For this reason, Jesus gives us this opposite but parallel truth: mercy—the virtue of mercy creates a balance in those who fight for human rights to prevail.

What is the reward for the merciful?

People who are merciful, in addition to being righteous, will, themselves, receive mercy. However, those who do not pity their brother will suffer judgment without mercy. Yes, we should love justice, but we must also love mercy. Why? Because someday we will need it. If we *sow* mercy and righteousness, we will *reap* the same in return.

The combination of these two virtues (righteousness and mercy) produces the third beatitude that compliments this second group: the pure in heart.

6. Blessed are the pure in heart

"⁸Blessed are the pure in heart, for they shall see God." Matthew 5.8

Who are the pure in heart?

Synthesis: The pure in heart are the men and women whose inner being is free of impure mixtures; without stain, uncorrupted, sincere, and genuine. They are people who were purified through events that shook their foundation. To be "shaken" is to experience great tribulation and adversity in life, and when this takes place, if the individual learns his lesson, his heart and soul will be cleansed.

What is the reward of the pure in heart?

The reward for the pure in heart is their ability to see God. Practicing righteousness, works of justice, fighting for people's rights to prevail, and at the same time staying merciful with those who do evil against us, will transform us into people of pure hearts. Best of all, it allows us to see how God works in our lives. Moreover, we will see Him in the lives of others, in our families, at our job, in our church, in the business world, in nature, in children, in the vision, in our dreams, in power, and in salvation. Those who are pure in heart will see God in *everything* they do.

People with impure hearts and minds cannot see God, be sensitive to His voice, nor discern when the Holy Spirit wants to guide them. The senses of the individual with an unsettled or troubled heart are contaminated by sin, lies, and impurities. Respectively, the pure in heart will see God, both spiritually and physically; they will witness His manifestation in their lives and in the lives of others.

What is the third group of beatitudes?

In this third group, Jesus' teaching challenges us to restore our relationships with our fellow brothers and sisters, while warning of the inevitable persecution that will come as a result of it. What a paradox to know we will be persecuted for His cause—the Savior of the world—and for doing what is right for others! Yet, that is how society repays those who choose not to conform to its desires, mentality, norms, and standards.

7. Blessed are the peacemakers

"⁹Blessed are the peacemakers, for they shall be called sons of God."
Matthew 5.9

Who are the peacemakers?

Thesis: Peacemakers create harmony among the people whose relationships are broken. Biblical peace is defined as the act of mending relationships that were hostile and to reconcile them, even if that means the peacemaker has to put his/her life in danger to accomplish it. To be a peacemaker does not mean there is tranquility, quietness, or rest; but rather, it is a *proactive* attitude that strives to restore hostile and broken relationships (Chapter six will cover the subject of peace in more detail). Peacemakers of the Kingdom is one who does whatever it takes to restore the relationships between fathers and sons, pastors and their congregation, employers and employees, the government and its people, and the relationship of one nation with another. Their desire is to bring harmony to every relationship at every level.

What is the reward for peacemakers?

Those who are actively striving to restore the peace in any hostile relationship will be called "sons of God." The Greek word for *son* is *huio* and it means: a mature son. In essence, Jesus said that those who bring peace and harmony into any broken relationship will be called a *mature son* of God. An important characteristic of a mature son is his readiness to receive his inheritance.

That was the first truth established by the third group. With it, God creates another parallel but opposite truth in order to bring balance and shape the character of Christ within man.

8. **Blessed (joyful) are those who are persecuted for the sake of righteousness**

"¹⁰Blessed are those who are persecuted for righteousness' sake, for theirs is the Kingdom of heaven." Matthew 5.10

Once again, we learn that establishing righteousness and the Kingdom of God on Earth will cause us to suffer persecution— antithesis. However, it is good to know that those who suffer persecution will also be called blessed. Peacemakers are persecuted because they bring harmony to a world full of dissension, argumentation, fighting, and conflict. When we do not conform to the world's established standards, values, comfort zones, securities, desires, fears, anxieties, and rewards, we will suffer persecution.

What is the reward for those who suffer persecution for the sake of righteousness?

The reward that comes with this virtue is the same as the one received by the poor in spirit: the Kingdom of God belongs to them. Every virtue and blessing of the Kingdom is available to everyone who gives up and sacrifices their sense of comfort, peace, tranquility, and security for the sake of righteousness. Their reward is eternal.

9. Blessed are those who are reviled and persecuted for Jesus' sake

"¹¹Blessed are you when they revile and persecute you, and say all kinds of evil against you falsely for My sake." Matthew 5.11

Synthesis: Seeking and establishing righteousness will cause us to suffer persecution. Inevitably, all peacemakers and those who identify themselves with Jesus will suffer persecution. He warned our persecutors would spread lies about us when they are unable to find anything to use against us.

To be *reviled* means to be harshly and ruthlessly criticized, rebuked, and censored—insulted, abused, scorned, or despised. Often, christians are criticized or censured because of our faith. The world tries to silence us because it does not want to hear the truth found in the Word of God. However, Jesus teaches that when we are reviled we are truly blessed because it draws a beautiful reward toward us.

What is the reward for those who are reviled for Jesus' sake?

"¹²Rejoice and be exceedingly glad, for great is your reward in heaven, for so they persecuted the prophets who were before you." Matthew 5.12

The reward in heaven is great for those who, instead of denying Christ or remaining stagnant and in a neutral position, are willing to give up their lives for the sake of the Kingdom of God and its righteousness. This reward brings great joy and happiness, and it creates a balance to counter the persecution suffered for being a peacemaker. We are happy warriors—we do not try to be happy, we simply *are*.

In conclusion, Jesus teaches that peacemakers are happy and blessed because they bring harmony to hostile relationships. Also, He teaches that wanting to do "whatever it takes" for the people's rights to prevail will bring persecution. In addition, He said we would be persecuted if and when we identify ourselves with Him and His Kingdom because His principles and values are contrary to the world's system. However, after stating such harsh truths, He also declared wonderful encouraging news that make us realize that every good thing we do will be rewarded in heaven and on Earth. Therefore, we must be ready to fight and establish the Kingdom on Earth and avoid being surprised by persecution. Jesus urges us to rejoice and be happy at all times because it is an antidote to our persecution.

Chapter 6

ESSENTIAL ELEMENTS THAT MAKE UP THE KINGDOM

Once, there was a man that received a bar of gold with an engraved seal of "18 carats" as payment for his labor. The bar shined like gold and its weight was correct, but as a precaution, the man took the bar to a jewelry store to have it appraised by an expert. There, the jeweler pulled out his instruments and started to study the item. In only a few minutes, and with complete certainty, he said, "This is not a bar of pure gold; it is a mixture of several materials." The engraving said it was pure gold, but the expert discovered its impurities.

The same happens today in our churches and religious circles. Many talk about the Kingdom. They teach on it, use its language, believe in God, attend church, and give their offerings. It is as if they also have an engraved seal stating their legitimacy, but inside, they are void of the Kingdom. In their hearts there is only loneliness and insecurities. They are thirsty for something different. This happens when the essential elements of the Kingdom are not present in their lives. The seal may be impressive, but if the church or individual does not contain the pure elements of the Kingdom, it is not the Kingdom. Consequently, what they practice is a dead religion that never satisfies the heart, regardless of what the religion is called.

Guided by the Holy Spirit, I will explain, in detail, the essential elements that make up the Kingdom of God and show you how to distinguish whether or not they are operating. Before we begin, let us first learn how to enter the Kingdom of God so these elements can legally operate in our lives.

How do we enter the Kingdom of God?

"³Jesus answered and said to him, "Most assuredly, I say to you, unless one is born again, he cannot see the Kingdom of God." ⁴Nicodemus said to

Him, "How can a man be born when he is old? Can he enter a second time into his mother's womb and be born?" ⁵Jesus answered, "Most assuredly, I say to you, unless one is born of water and the Spirit, he cannot enter the Kingdom of God." John 3.3-5

Before saying this, in the beginning of His ministry, Jesus exhorted the people using two key words:

❖ **Repent:** a total change of mind and lifestyle
❖ **Believe in the gospel:** accept the good news of the Kingdom

What does it mean to be born again?

The expression **born again** is the Greek word *gennao* which means: to be begotten or fathered. In other words, to be born again in the Spirit means to be begotten or fathered by the Holy Spirit—this is the only path that leads to the Kingdom of God.

How does this process take place? The Word of God teaches there are three stages that must take place for the Kingdom to come into our lives and for the Holy Spirit to beget us. These are:

We must be born again to enter the Kingdom of God,
and this can only be accomplished through the Holy Spirit.

❖ **The Kingdom is at hand**

"¹⁷From that time Jesus began to preach and to say, "Repent, for the Kingdom of heaven is at hand." Matthew 4.17

This is the stage where someone has just shared the good news of the gospel with us. At that moment, the good news stands at the door of our lives, but it waits for our decision to allow it to enter. The Kingdom comes, and we must accept or decline it. Many people reject the Kingdom and continue to live their lives without any change. Others receive it and their lives are changed and transformed, forever. When we open the doors of our hearts and allow Jesus to come in, the new birth takes place. It is in that precise moment of acceptance that we are begotten or fathered by the Holy Spirit of God and born again into His Kingdom. When that occurs, the elements of His government begin affecting our lives and modifying everything around us.

When an individual genuinely repents, everything that derived from their independence of God will end: wretchedness, depression, and loneliness become a thing of the past because joy, peace, righteousness, and the power of the Kingdom get activated and become effective in their new life. Mankind must open up its heart to the Kingdom of God. If you have not done it, I am sure the opportunity to bring you closer to the Kingdom of God will arise. When this happens, open your heart and you will be born again. Your life will be completely transformed!

Who cannot enter the Kingdom of God?

"[9]Do you not know that the unrighteous will not inherit the Kingdom of God? Do not be deceived. Neither fornicators, nor idolaters, nor adulterers, nor homosexuals, nor sodomites, [10]nor thieves, nor covetous, nor drunkards, nor revilers, nor extortioners will inherit the Kingdom of God." 1 Corinthians 6.9, 10

The Word is very specific by giving us a list of the people who cannot enter or inherit the Kingdom of God. For the most part, these people rejected Jesus and want to continue practicing their sinful lifestyle and refuse to repent of their sins.

❖ **The Kingdom is within us**

"[20]...the Kingdom of God does not come with signs to be observed or with visible display, [21]nor will people say, Look! Here [it is]! or, See, [it is] there! For behold, the Kingdom of God is within you [in your hearts] and among you [surrounding you]." Luke 17.20, 21—AMP

In this stage, the Kingdom of God and God Himself come to abide in us. God places His Word in our hearts and the Holy Spirit gives us the power to experience it. Now, wherever we go, the Kingdom goes with us and becomes an agent of change for those who need to hear the good news. We begin to see the elements of the Kingdom operating in our lives and influencing others to seek God and lead them out of the kingdom of darkness and into His marvelous light—Jesus!

❖ The Kingdom of God is upon us

"28But if I cast out demons by the Spirit of God, surely the Kingdom of God has come upon you." Matthew 12.28

This is the stage in which the Holy Spirit brings a visible and supernatural manifestation of the Kingdom's power that dwells *in* us. Examples of this manifestation are: rebuking demons, healing the sick, performing miracles, or any other supernatural manifestation of God's power.

At this point, it is important to remember that Jesus, the absolute King of the Kingdom, made Himself human, died on the cross, and was raised from the dead to save mankind and give us the opportunity to be born again and live in His Kingdom. With this in mind, we can now fully discuss the essential elements that make up the Kingdom.

Essential elements that make up the Kingdom of God

"17...for the Kingdom of God is not eating and drinking, but righteousness and peace and joy in the Holy Spirit." Romans 14.17

1. Righteousness

It is extremely important to understand that righteousness is one of the most relevant elements of the heavenly government. Since the subject of righteousness was well covered in previous chapters, it will not be covered here, but I will, once again, remind you that it is the most essential element of the Kingdom, and it was part of the main message that Jesus delivered on Earth.

2. Peace

The apostle Paul taught that peace is an important component of the Kingdom. Isaiah also spoke on the subject.

"17The work of righteousness will be peace, and the effect of righteousness, quietness and assurance forever." Isaiah 32.17

Peace is what comes from performing works of righteousness. It consists in leading all men to salvation, restoring or making sure the rights of the individual prevail, performing works of social justice, and impartial governing. This Scripture is very powerful! The outcome of successfully accomplishing the rights of individuals to prevail is peace and security for our society. However, this is only possible through the reinstatement of God's government, on Earth. This must take place first; otherwise, regardless of how hard a leader works to bring peace to his nation, it will be very difficult to accomplish unless he incorporates the principles of the Kingdom into his plan of action—because everything that is good comes from God. Man cannot produce anything that is good or effective on his own, and the same happens in every aspect of man's existence and the universe.

Peace and security come upon a society
when the Kingdom of God is established.
Any human effort to gain any of the two
will only create new conflicts.

What is peace?

Peace, in Hebrew, is the word *shalom;* in Greek it is the word *eirene,* and both mean serenity, quietness, rest, strength, tranquility, the end of hostilities or war. However, if we were to focus on the word *eirene,* the definition given would only reflect a part of its full meaning.

Eirene essentially means to restore a hostile relationship in such a way that both parts will be perfectly reconciled and live together in a relationship of true love. Peace has little to do with simple tranquility or quietness; it means to reconcile, restore, or mend broken relationships—to bring harmony between the parties involved, but most importantly between God and man.

During the times when the New Testament was written, the word *eirene* was used in connection with medicine as a term to describe the healing or restoration of a broken bone. When a broken bone reconnects, it becomes stronger, harder, and more resistant than its original state. A bone that heals this way will never break in the same place twice. The doctors refer to the new bone as *cayo oseo*. This new bone is more resistant and stronger than the original bone. Therefore, it was accustomed to say that the bone was "in peace"—*eirene*. Similarly, a peacemaker is one who reconciles and restores broken relationships.

Every one of us, at one time or another, have broken off a relationship—have broken a bone in the body of Christ and/or a bone in our family. Thus, God is raising peacemakers so they can restore the broken relationships among nations, family members, and between fathers and sons. Jesus, the King of God's government, by His own free will, surrendered His life in order to restore our relationship with the Father. As a result, our relationship is stronger than ever before! Yes, our broken relationship was restored and brought to peace—*eirene*.

"20...and by Him to reconcile all things to Himself, by Him, whether things on Earth or things in heaven, having made peace through the blood of His cross." Colossians 1.20

A totally innocent God came in human form and surrendered His life as a sacrifice in order to make peace with all men. Jesus was a peacemaker and used a powerful description for those who would become peacemakers:

"9Blessed are the peacemakers, for they shall be called sons of God." Matthew 5.9

In those days, men were called by the dominant quality in their character. For instance, John and James were called the "sons of thunder." Likewise, peacemakers will be called, "sons of God" because they do the same as what God does: They conquer evil with good and destroy hate with love.

Are you willing to mend broken relationships? Are you willing to overcome evil with good? Have you broken a bone in a relationship, lately?

From this point of view, peace means to restore a hostile relationship; to reconcile it even to the point of giving up one's life. This is what the Kingdom is all about: to make the rights of the individual prevail and to restore the relationship between God and mankind, and amongst men. When these two elements (peace and righteousness) of the Kingdom line up in order, the third element takes place:

3. Joy

Joy is a spiritual force that makes us happy regardless of external circumstances.

"17...for the Kingdom of God is not eating and drinking, but righteousness and peace and joy in the Holy Spirit." Romans 14.17

Righteousness brings us salvation, it makes the rights of individuals prevail, it provides works of social justice, and it leads to an impartial government. Righteousness is peace in the hearts of men. Peace and righteousness in one's life bring an uncut joy.

"11These things I have spoken to you, that My joy may remain in you, and that your joy may be full." John 15.11

The joy that comes from the Kingdom of God is not based on temporal things, brief moments, or good or bad circumstances that take place around us. This joy is the result of having a beautiful relationship with God the Father, and with everyone around us.

It is safe to conclude, then, that the world's system offers a fragile and unstable alternative to justice, peace, and joy. This world and its systems is not capable or powerful enough to assure these virtues to mankind. The world does not govern itself, but it is subject to curses and the kingdom of darkness. Therefore, even a genuine desire for justice, peace, and joy, cannot do it; these are results impossible to gain outside the Kingdom of God.

Previously, we saw how the first elements that make up the Kingdom of God are correlated to relationships, not only with God but also amongst humans. Therefore, it is no surprise that psychologists acknowledge righteousness, peace, and joy as basic needs for every human being. Yet, we have witnessed that all these elements can only be found within a superior, unshakeable, strong, and eternal Kingdom—the Kingdom of God.

The plan of God for man is to bring His Kingdom, give him peace, joy, and righteousness through a close relationship with Him. King Jesus is the peacemaker that restored this relationship, and worship is the way we express our love, submission, and total surrender to a perfect King who is full of love and power.

4. Fatherhood

God designed the church, society, politics, the government, the family, and all other human relationships so they can operate under the pattern of fatherhood. This is an absolute fundamental of the government of God. Everything that operates under the fatherhood of God is within His Kingdom. Hence, any organism that operates under this principle has the Kingdom in place.

Fatherhood is the perfect balancing ingredient within the absolute government of God because it encloses His immense love for us.

"15...from whom the whole family in heaven and Earth is named..."
Ephesians 3.15

The Greek word for **family** is *patria;* the word *patriarch* comes from this root word, and it means: someone's sphere of fatherhood. Biblically speaking, without a father there is no family.

Paternity is one of the most important elements of the Kingdom of God. Today, we have an orphaned generation—orphaned because of absentee fathers or men who lack paternal character. This is the main reason why we live in a society void of values; why young people join gangs, practice a homosexual lifestyle, and commit crimes. They grew up without fathers to impart into them true fatherhood, and even when the father figure was physically present, he was not necessarily capable of carrying out his role.

After salvation, the greatest need
of a human being is to have a father.

Society was designed by God to function under the pattern of fatherhood. Accordingly, we cannot say we are a Kingdom church if we do not practice this principle. Today, we do not need more charismatic politicians, professionals, or pastors who are hired but not called. We need men with the Father's heart—apostles, pastors, presidents, politicians, and fathers with a true paternal heart (God's heart).

How does God solve the *absence of fatherhood* problem?

"17He will also go before Him in the spirit and power of Elijah, 'to turn the hearts of the fathers to the children,' and the disobedient to the wisdom of the just, to make ready a people prepared for the Lord."
Luke 1.17

Through Jesus and His unshakeable Kingdom, God is sending out the spirit of Elijah to restore fatherhood. The Kingdom of God consists of righteousness, peace, and joy, but it cannot exist without fatherhood; thus, every believer needs to have an intimate relationship with the Heavenly Father and cry out, "*Abba, Father!*"

"⁶And because you are sons, God has sent forth the Spirit of His Son into your hearts, crying out, "Abba, Father!" Galatians 4.6

Once more, we have proven that the Kingdom of God entirely depends on relationships. In this case, fatherhood consists of having a father/son relationship with our Heavenly Father; one that has intimacy and mutual respect.

Without the revelation of fatherhood, one cannot understand the Kingdom of God. However, once we understand this relationship, it becomes easy to live under the totalitarian government of a loving Father, and subsequently, we begin to enjoy its inherent benefits which include joy, security, rest, and protection. If you have never experienced this intimate relationship with God, to get it, you must first want it with all your heart.

One of the reasons why the Holy Spirit came was to reveal the Father to us. In Galatians, Paul mentions how the spirit of adoption, through which we cry out *Abba* or *Daddy*, is the same spirit that cries out, *"You are my beloved son!"* Receive your adoption by faith. You do not have to be an orphan. The Father loves you, and that is why He brought His Kingdom into our lives and why we are His beloved children!

If we preach the Kingdom and fail to teach on the fatherhood of God, it can be easily mistaken for a type of severe or harsh regime. However, when we look at it from a beloved son's point of view, we are able to joyfully obey our father because we know our Father is good and infinitely wise. It no longer seems like a regimen but a relationship. This drastically changes the meaning of this relationship and the concept of submission, dependence, absolute obedience, and totalitarianism.

Jesus did not find it hard to live in the Kingdom. On the contrary, it was an absolute joy for Him because His love-based relationship with His Father was absolutely glorious. Both understood each other, completely. They both had the same vision and were willing to pay the price to reach it.

Before going ahead to the next element of the Kingdom, please, take a moment to analyze your relationship with God using the answers to the following questions as guidance: Do you strive to know the Father the same way that Jesus knew Him? Do you have a loving relationship with Him? Do you see yourself as a true son? Have you received the spirit of adoption?

This generation suffers a very unfortunate problem: They lack a strong and healthy relationship with their biological father. Consequently, many continue to be clueless on how to be a good father and/or how to be a good child. This lack of knowledge hinders them from establishing a relationship with their Heavenly Father. Further, because their relationship with their natural father is the only example of relationship they have, they base their decision to approach and see God as a Father, on a false premise of fatherhood and sonship; thus, in most instances, the only way to know Him is through the Holy Spirit. He teaches and reveals the heart of the Father. If you still have not met the Father, ask the Holy Spirit, and He will reveal the Father to you.

Fatherhood is one of the fundamental elements of the Kingdom of God. We can say that fatherhood is the beginning and the end of the Kingdom—the reason for being and the effect of the same: A paternal relationship between God and man existing in a perfect and eternal Kingdom. The most important point to make here is that the relationship with the Heavenly Father is available for you!

5. Love

The Kingdom depends on another vital element for its existence, and this element is also one of its essential fundamentals: love.

In connection with the previous element, love is a virtue belonging to a father that gives himself, unconditionally, to his children.

"16For God so loved the world that He gave His only begotten Son, that whoever believes in Him should not perish but have everlasting life." John 3.16

Fatherhood does not exist without love; and love is incomplete if it is not applied with the heart of a father.

Our Heavenly Father loves us so much that He sent His son to die for us and to take our place. Even when we lived in our sin, He reconciled us to Him. He restored the relationship between us and God. Jesus loves us with the same love that the Father loves Him.

"9As the Father loved Me, I also have loved you; abide in My love. 10If you keep My commandments, you will abide in My love, just as I have kept My Father's commandments and abide in His love." John 15.9, 10

I believe there are many things we can say about love, but the most important thing to understand is that the Kingdom consists in living a life of love for God and others. We cannot say that the Kingdom lives in us when we fail to walk in love.

6. Order

"40...let all things be done decently and in order." 1 Corinthians 14.40

What does *order* mean?

Order is the Greek word *taxis*; it means: an arrangement; a fixed succession observing a fixed time; the post, rank, or position which one holds in civic or military affairs. Order can be found in everything and every aspect of the Kingdom. Order is an important element needed to establish the Kingdom of God and a condition for it to remain in place. The opposite of order is confusion. In the absence of order, there will always be confusion, and God cannot dwell under such conditions.

"33...for God is not the author of confusion but of peace, as in all the churches of the saints." 1 Corinthians 14.33

Who is responsible for establishing order in the body of Christ?

Apostles under the direction of our Lord, Jesus, are responsible for establishing and enforcing respect for the Kingdom's order, be it in local churches and /or across the world.

"34...but if anyone is hungry, let him eat at home, lest you come together for judgment. And the rest I will set in order when I come." 1 Corinthians 11.34

God creates everything with a purpose. He is not a God of confusion. In everything He does, He always exemplifies order— organization oriented towards reaching the purpose of its Kingdom. As the Father of all created things, God placed order in: authority, time, the home, priesthood, ministry, the doctrine, and leadership. He established order to build, execute, and begin to organize our path, steps, and destiny; to bring order to days, weeks, years, and centuries, and to make sure there is order in every life cycle of life. God also established order in His Kingdom to eliminate chaos and create blessings. Therefore, order is a fundamental element in the Kingdom. If we allow this element to operate in our lives, we will be much more effective and be able to reach our goals and destiny.

7. Obedience, submission, and authority

At the beginning of the book, we learned that the heavenly realm obeys God, completely. The King is a loving father whom we obey, not out of obligation but out of love, knowing that in His absolute totalitarianism we find absolute liberty.

"⁸...though He was a Son, yet He learned obedience by the things which He suffered." Hebrews 5.8

Jesus, as the Son of God, had to learn to obey His Father. If *He* had to learn, imagine how much more we need to learn. The Kingdom of God cannot be established if His authority, will, Word, and commandments are not obeyed. The Kingdom of God can be found wherever the principle of obedience is in operation. The opposite of obedience is rebellion or independence; this was the sin that caused Adam to lose the Kingdom.

The only way to gain authority in the Kingdom is by submitting to authorities and serving God and our neighbors. Any place the Kingdom is established, we find an executive head with authority given by God, whom the people obey and submit to, not out of obligation but out of love.

8. Humility

"³...and said, "Assuredly, I say to you, unless you are converted and become as little children, you will by no means enter the Kingdom of heaven. ⁴Therefore whoever humbles himself as this little child is the greatest in the Kingdom of Heaven." Matthew 18.3, 4

What is true humility? Genuine humility is to be aware of one's essence, value, and identity in God. A humble person is one who recognizes, without exaggeration or underestimating, who he is in his job, ministry, family, and anywhere.

Humility is not hiding who we are.
It is being and saying without adding or taking away;
always with the understanding that it is not
by our own merit but by the gift of God.

Illustration: I consider myself to be a good leader. I do not think I am the best, but I know I am not the worst. I am good. Humility means recognizing what we are from a Biblical standpoint—not according to our way of thinking or how the world perceives us.

At the same time, the word **humble** means or describes a person that lacks arrogance and pride. One who is easy to teach, easy to shape, and who easily asks to be forgiven when he makes a mistake. A person who gives God the credit and honor and who also honors people when credit is due. A humble person bows his head when he offends others and knows how to repent and ask for forgiveness. He even knows how to take a step back when it is not necessary to do so. This person depends totally on God and is consumed with the passion to do His perfect will.

Jesus is our perfect role model

"8...and being found in appearance as a man, He humbled Himself and became obedient to the point of death, even the death of the cross." Philippians 2.8

Jesus taught that all the resources of the Kingdom are available to those who are humble. When we study the elements that make up the Kingdom, we can conclude that almost all of them have to do with relationships with both, God and men. This leads to the following extremely important conclusion: The Kingdom of God is a kingdom of relationships; thus, since the Kingdom is found within a place or individual, we must be able to see its elements operating in them. Once the Kingdom is established, those who are truly touched by it will begin to live and walk in those principles. Our job, as people under God's government, is to preach, believe, and extend the Kingdom on Earth, and win every nation for Christ.

The Kingdom is established
through covenant relationships.

"47 Again, the Kingdom of heaven is like a dragnet that was cast into the sea and gathered some of every kind." Matthew 13.47

The Kingdom is in us, upon us, and all around us. Let us take it all in! Let us practice righteousness and fight to see the rights of the individual prevail. Let us ask God to give us hunger and thirst for His righteousness. Let us love justice, hate iniquity, and do what is right towards our fellow men. We should seek peace, establish peace, and restore or mend broken relationships. Doing such things will create in us a joyful heart that does not depend on external circumstances but on the Kingdom that is already rooted in our lives.

We need to ask the Holy Spirit to teach us and reveal to us the fatherhood of God; to fill us with His love and teach us to be obedient and submissive with one another whereby we can demonstrate a genuine, not fake, humility. We should do such things so we can walk like Jesus walked—loving our neighbors. We must bring Kingdom order into every activity we perform, and in our church, family, and business. Otherwise, we will experience confusion. When we are subject to order, we can easily and joyfully obey and submit to the will of God.

Today, make the decision to walk in humility—with a humble mentality—following the perfect role model. We should be open to learning, to the new things the Holy Spirit wants to show us, to new ways of thinking, and always recognizing that what we have and who we are we owe to God.

This chapter only covered the first part of what makes up the Kingdom which has to do with relationships. In the next chapter, we will cover the second part—the supernatural.

The order of the Kingdom
brings joy to our lives and helps us
correctly relate with others.

Chapter 7

A Supernatural Kingdom

When Dr. T. L. Osborn visited our church as a guest speaker in a leadership conference, he confessed something that touched my heart, deeply. He said, "When my wife Daisy and I were very young, we visited India as missionaries—we wanted to share the gospel with the Muslims and Hindus. To our surprise, we were unable to convince them that Jesus is the Son of God and that He had been raised from the dead because they demanded proof that what we said was true. We shared many Bible verses, but they had their own bible, the Koran. Muslims believe the Koran is the word of God which was spoken through the prophet Muhammad. Both books are precious—they said—both with golden rims and delicate pages, but they also asked, "Which of the two treasures the Word of God?" We were unable to prove that ours was the true Word of God because, at the time, we did not fully understand the power of faith or knew that miracles were the signs that make the Word true. We did not understand that the Kingdom of God is a supernatural Kingdom, and we returned to America feeling ashamed and defeated.

Sometime later, we had a supernatural revelation of Jesus, in our room. When this took place, we returned to India with the power of the supernatural. From that point on, wherever we go, we have been able to prove that God is all-powerful who performs miracles, healing, signs, and wonders, and that Jesus is alive because He was raised from the dead. Jesus was not "another great prophet," but God, "made flesh."

After hearing his testimony, the Lord showed me that His Kingdom has two parts and that one without the other is not enough to reach the lost. We need both parts:

- **Relationships:** In the previous chapter, we learned about right-eousness, peace, fatherhood, and love among other things. Making it clear the Kingdom of God is founded on relationships.

- **Power:** This is the supernatural part of the Kingdom that operates under the omnipotence of its King. Power, is what this chapter is all about…

The difference between the Kingdom that is preached and the one that is established lies in the action that supersedes the words and where theory transforms into a practical and visible demonstration of His intrinsic power. This is a violent cross over that most people are not willing to make because it demands a greater level of faith, commitment, and risk. Further, it is also one that demands for a greater price to be paid. Most religions of the world say nice things but they lack the power to change anyone. In Dr. T. L. Osborn's testimony, we see that the difference in his ministry was marked when he returned to India with more than mere words. He returned with the visible and genuine demonstration of the gospel's power. Subsequently, the sick were healed and the demon-possessed were delivered, to mention a few. The signs and wonders that followed his ministry enabled him to prove his message of the gospel was true, that the Bible is the Word of the only true God, and that Jesus is also the Savior for Hindus and Muslims. It does not matter how strong a tradition, religion, or culture might be, when the power of God descends and manifests, every human argument is destroyed and left void.

Regardless of how strong a tradition, religion,
or culture might be, when the power of God manifests,
every argument is destroyed.

In the Old Testament, when someone spoke about the God of Israel, every town and nation feared Him because they knew He lived in the invisible realm, not the visible world. Contrary to the gods they worshipped, who were made out of wood and mud, the God of Israel was understood to be supernatural. Accordingly, the word Kingdom can also be translated as: supernatural. Jesus came to express the supernatural power of His Kingdom in the natural realm. Therefore, the Kingdom of God does not consist solely on relationships, but also in the supernaturally manifested *power*—also known as the second component of the Kingdom.

"²⁰For the Kingdom of God is not in word but in power." 1 Corinthians 4.20

What type of power is this?

- The power to *be*
- The power to *do* (take action)

In the Old Testament, there is an enormous group of Greek words that come from the same root word but have different connotations. However, all the words seek to enrich and transmit, in words, a supernatural quality (not human) that can only belong to a deity.

"⁴⁹Behold, I send the Promise of My Father upon you; but tarry in the city of Jerusalem until you are endued with power from on high." Luke 24.49

The word **power** derives from the Greek words *dunamis, dynastes, dynatos,* and the verbs *dynamoo* and *dynateo.* All these words are translated as power and appear over three hundred times throughout Scripture. Let us learn the three most significant meanings:

❖ **Power:** This word can be translated as power of force, strength, or the ability to do something and carry it out all the way until its completion.

"¹³I can do all things through Christ who strengthens me."
Philippians 4.13

The word *dunamis* is used twice in this verse which means that it could, literally, be written the following way: *"I am powerful enough to do all things in Christ who enables me with His power."*

❖ **Able:** this next verse can also be translated as *powerfully capable* which means that God is able.

"²⁰Now to Him who is able to do exceedingly abundantly above all that we ask or think, according to the power that works in us." Ephesians 3.20

God is *able to do exceedingly abundantly above all that we ask or think, according to the power that works in us.* Every time it specifically describes what we can do, it also places us in the same category as God. Of course, this can only take place after the Kingdom has come upon us through the Holy Spirit. Without His power, we can do nothing. It is worth noting that I am not stating that we are God, but that we are, however, powerful because Jesus gives us His power.

❖ **Possible:** This is the same word in Greek.

"²⁶But Jesus looked at them and said to them, "With men this is impossible, but with God all things are <u>possible</u>." Matthew 19.26

Everything is possible to him who believes.

"²³Jesus said to him, "If you can believe, all things are <u>possible</u> to him who believes." Mark 9.23

The Bible also teaches that all things that are possible for God are also possible for us. In other words, if God can do something, then, without a shadow of a doubt, the believer can also do it, as long as he is properly connected to Him, is full of the Holy Spirit, and is rooted in His Kingdom.

When a person enters the Kingdom through the born-again experience, they receive the power to *be* and to *do*, regardless of religion. Men seek power in their own strength but are unable to acquire it because that power can only be found in God. Most people seek power to change the circumstances in their lives.

Everyone wants to have control and dominion over their surrounding circumstances because having things out of control causes insecurity.

Countless people seek power to make themselves wealthy, good, powerful, intelligent, recognized, or famous. They want the power to change their personality or character but are unable to find it. The world is in constant search mode. People seek what they lack in religion, traditions, and disciplines. They want the power to change their circumstances.

"¹⁸And when Simon saw that through the laying on of the apostles' hands the Holy Spirit was given, he offered them money, ¹⁹saying, "Give me this power also, that anyone on whom I lay hands may receive the Holy Spirit." Acts 8.18, 19

Simon was a magician who wanted the power of God without entering the Kingdom or believing in Jesus. However, that power is only available to those who believe in Jesus as their Lord and who enter the Kingdom through the new birth and the repentance of their sins.

The supernatural is the seal of the Kingdom of God

The life of Jesus is characterized by the supernatural seal of the Kingdom. When we enter the Kingdom and meet Jesus, His Holy Spirit gives us the power to modify our circumstances, the power to change the bad or dark aspects in our character, and the power to change our behavior and decisions. If Jesus lives in our hearts and we are full of the Holy Spirit, the supernatural will always rise to the surface. Jesus had the power over nature and the physical laws. This was proven when He calmed the storm, walked on water, transformed the water into wine, and many other times.

No one likes to be controlled by others. Men need to be in control of their own lives and circumstances, making the power of the Kingdom a necessity. Man was created to have lordship over all things created by God, except people. People followed Jesus because they were drawn to the manifested benefits of the Kingdom's power, especially because, through them, they were able to see that He had dominion over all things.

People may believe they can find power in witchcraft, the occult, religion, business, sciences, or politics, but that is not the case. True power can only be experienced when one is rooted in the Kingdom of God—it *powerfully enables* us to *perform* miracles, to *make* our business situations turn out right, and to *make* all things possible, in order to be different than others and be the same as Jesus.

> The Kingdom of God is not just words:
> it is the power to be, the power to do,
> and the power to take action.

The only place where Jesus did not perform miracles was in His own land because of the people's unbelief: Doubt is the main obstacle that keeps the Kingdom from manifesting itself.

"⁵⁸Now He did not do many mighty works there because of their unbelief." Matthew 13.58

For thirty years, the people saw Jesus as one of their own and never saw Him perform a miracle. They were familiarized with Jesus the carpenter—the one without power. Therefore, Jesus, the miracle maker, was a stranger to them. Many Christians grow up in churches where Christ is nothing more than a religion; where He is dead. They do not know Him as the Christ, the all-powerful One, the maker of miracles, signs, and wonders. Have you ever witnessed miracles take place in your church? How many times?

What are the characteristics of this supernatural Kingdom?

Up to this point, we understand the Kingdom of God to be different and superior to other kingdoms, but to expand on the subject and begin to fully live in it, we need to know its characteristics:

1. **The laws of the Kingdom of God are superior to the laws in other kingdoms.**

Jesus lived on Earth according to the laws of the Kingdom of God and not to the laws of the natural kingdom; hence, He had dominion over time, space, matter, Earth, gravity, death, sickness, water, storms, the wind, and demons—He had dominion over all things. The difference between Him and us is the type of laws He followed. For instance:

- **Dominion over matter**

    "[17]And they said to Him, "We have here only five loaves and two fish." [18]He said, "Bring them here to Me." [19]Then He commanded the multitudes to sit down on the grass. And He took the five loaves and the two fish, and looking up to heaven, He blessed and broke and gave the loaves to the disciples; and the disciples gave to the multitudes. [20]So they all ate and were filled, and they took up twelve baskets full of the fragments that remained. [21]Now those who had eaten were about five thousand men, besides women and children."
    Matthew 14.17-21

    The laws of any kingdom on Earth, including the laws of the kingdom of darkness, point to the fact that one plus one equals two. These kingdoms are governed by the natural laws of mathematics, but in the case of Jesus, that law did not work because He operated under a superior law of multiplication which resulted in abundance.

- **Dominion over the forces of nature**

    "[35]On the same day, when evening had come, He said to them, "Let us cross over to the other side." [36]Now when they had left the multitude, they took Him along in the boat as He was. And other little boats were also with Him. [37]And a great windstorm arose, and the waves beat into the boat, so that it was already filling. [38]But He was in the stern, asleep on a

pillow. And they awoke Him and said to Him, "Teacher, do You not care that we are perishing?" [39]Then He arose and rebuked the wind, and said to the sea, "Peace, be still!" And the wind ceased and there was a great calm. [40]But He said to them, "Why are you so fearful? How is it that you have no faith?" [41]And they feared exceedingly, and said to one another, "Who can this be, that even the wind and the sea obey Him!"
Mark 4.35-41

The laws of nature were defeated by the laws of the Kingdom of God. Creation is not subject to man, but it is subject to the laws of the Kingdom. Jesus exercised His authority over all creation and the storm had to obey His word.

• Dominion over death

"[22]...beginning from the baptism of John to that day when He was taken up from us, one of these must become a witness with us of His resurrection." [23]And they proposed two: Joseph called Barsabas, who was surnamed Justus, and Matthias. [24]And they prayed and said, "You, O Lord, who know the hearts of all, show which of these two You have chosen."
Acts 1.22-24

Now we understand why Jesus was able to rise from the dead. He used a superior law that defeats the curse of the law by which all men must die.

Death is powerless against those
who are redeemed from the law and live under grace.

• Dominion over the physical laws

"[38]So he commanded the chariot to stand still. And both Philip and the eunuch went down into the water, and he baptized him. [39]Now when they came up out of the water, the Spirit of

the Lord caught Philip away, so that the eunuch saw him no more; and he went on his way rejoicing. ⁴⁰But Philip was found at Azotus. And passing through, he preached in all the cities till he came to Caesarea." Acts 8.38-40

Phillip broke the physical laws that operate over gravity, matter, time, and space. The Holy Spirit transported him from one place to another in the blinking of an eye. What a powerful experience! The apostles were equipped to the same as Jesus did. As a matter of fact, Jesus used this dominion several times after His resurrection. Today, we can do the same if we believe in Him and His Kingdom.

Illustration: The following is the testimony of a preacher of the gospel who was sent by the Lord to a mission in India. God instructed him to go to the airport and wait for his flight. The missionary followed His instructions verbatim. He arrived at the airline and waited for a long time, but nothing happened; finally, he decided to go to the Men's Room. When he returned, he found himself in an airport in India. He had the same experience that Phillip had: he was transported by the Holy Spirit! The physical laws that operate on Earth were violated and replaced by the supernatural laws of the Kingdom. In Scripture, these extraordinary events are referred to as "powers of the age to come."

"⁵...and have tasted the good word of God and the powers of the age to come..." Hebrews 6.5

- **Dominion over sickness and demons**

"²³...Jesus went about all Galilee, teaching in their synagogues, preaching the gospel of the Kingdom, and healing all kinds of sickness and all kinds of disease among the people. ²⁴Then His fame went throughout all Syria; and they brought to Him all sick people who were afflicted with various diseases and

torments, and those who were demon-possessed, epileptics, and paralytics; and He healed them." Matthew 4.23, 24

Illustration: John G. Lake was a powerful apostle of the faith sent by God to Africa. During his time in Africa, he had to pray for many who were dying with a sickness called "bubonic plague." It was a deadly disease transmitted by touch which could kill a human being in a matter of hours. John G. Lake recalls he would take the hands of the sick, pray for them, and they would get healed, without anything happening to him. Why? The laws of the Kingdom are superior to the laws of the land and those of any other kingdom.

- **Dominion over gravity**

"26 And when the disciples saw Him walking on the sea, they were troubled, saying, "It is a ghost!" And they cried out for fear." Matthew 14.26

What is God's message to us? Everything we have learned demonstrates that we can experience the exact same power that raised Jesus from the dead. We can have dominion over poverty, sickness, demons, matter, time, and all those things that were once beyond our reach. We can be what God wants us to be because He gives us the power to accomplish it.

God's children have the power of the resurrection to change any situation contrary to God's will.

The element of the supernatural is what makes the Kingdom of God superior to other kingdoms on Earth. This power makes the Kingdom of Heaven superior to the kingdom of darkness and every other system operating throughout the world, today. There are countless passages found in Scripture that tell of the supernatural quality of

God and the superiority of His Kingdom. Why? Because it is unshakeable, eternal, and beyond the boundaries of this world.

"[36]Jesus answered, "My Kingdom is not of this world. If My Kingdom were of this world, My servants would fight, so that I should not be delivered to the Jews; but now My Kingdom is not from here." John 18.36

When the laws of the Kingdom supersede natural laws and a miracle takes place, all argumentation and human philosophy comes to an end—*a tangible miracle ends any intellectual discussion.* In scientific language, any empirical experience confirms or refutes a theory. In this case, the empirical experience of a miracle refutes human theories and confirms the Word of God. Actions always speak louder than words.

A miracle ends any intellectual discussion.

The difference between the Kingdom of God and religion, including the Christian religion, is that the government or Kingdom of God consists not only in word but also in power. Religion does not change anyone; it has no life or power capable of producing peace or joy. Religion is bondage incapable of providing the power that is needed to live as a son of God. There are no churches mentioned in the New Testament that were founded on anything other than the power of signs, wonders, miracles, and the expulsion of demons. Churches will only prosper and change their direction when the Kingdom is established.

2. **The Kingdom of God only operates in eternity; it is not restricted by time.**

Eternity is a *state of being* where time does not exist. When God created the Earth, He established time for the benefit of man because, being in a physical body, he needed to be subject to time. Eternity could be analyzed in three ways: past eternity, present eternity, and future eternity. At some point in this eternity, God established time for man to live by it.

The Kingdom is not subject to time; it operates above it in the realm of eternity. Therefore, to operate in its laws, we must learn to live differently. People who live according to Kingdom laws are free from the restrictions of earthly laws.

What type of currency is used in the Kingdom of God?

The "currency" needed to gain access to the supernatural Kingdom of God is: faith. The system of God operates by faith. Consequently, to live on Earth as if we were living in heaven, we must walk and live by faith. The same must be applied in eternity because faith operates above time. When we live according to Kingdom laws, we enter the sphere of the eternal, where hours, days, or years do not exist. God does not have a beginning or an end. He does not exist according to time as we know it because time is also part of His creation; it had a beginning and an end. This means that once time fulfills its purpose for existing, it will cease to exist. Time has an expiration date. We, on the other hand, will live in eternity!

"⁶...and swore by Him who lives forever and ever, who created heaven and the things that are in it, the Earth and the things that are in it, and the sea and the things that are in it, that there should be delay no longer..." Revelation 10.6

God's children received a measure of faith through the new birth, not only to operate in both worlds, the visible and the invisible, but also to avoid time becoming a limitation.

What is faith?

Let us take a brief look at the meaning of faith. Faith is not hope because hope has to do with the future; it does, however, *begin* with hope. Faith is not knowledge because knowledge means to judge all things through natural perception of the natural senses—touch, taste, smell, sight, and hearing.

Faith operates in the dimension of the spirit, not in the five natural senses. Knowledge is not faith because when we have the knowledge it is already too late for faith to take over. Faith is not something we assume can come to pass. If faith is not hope or knowledge, then what is faith?

Faith *is…*

"But without faith it is impossible to please Him, for he who comes to God must believe that He is, and that He is a rewarder of those who diligently seek Him." Hebrews 11.6

God *is…*

Faith is always present; it touches the eternal. God *is*: "I am that I am." He is the One that was, *is*, and always will be.

There are two worlds:

- **The spiritual world.** This world is discerned in the spirit, and it abides in the realm of faith.

- **The physical world.** This world is perceived through the five senses.

When we move in the spiritual realm, we have no tangible evidence of it; it is an internal, not physical nor intellectual knowing.

There are four dimensions in the natural world in which we live:

❖ Longitude
❖ Depth
❖ Time
❖ Space

People define eternity as "the wholeness of time or a very long time." However, eternity cannot be measured by time because it is an unconceivable concept for us capture.

When an object is launched at approximately the speed of light (186,000 miles per second), time begins to disappear. When we reach the speed of light, time becomes static and the aging process in things and people comes to a halt. Eternity means to live at the same level of energy as the speed of light.

Illustration: If a group of people board a spaceship traveling at 150,000 miles per second, when they return to Earth, even though 20 Earth years have passed, the group of people will physically be the same age as when they left; it will be as if they had never left. When they exit the spaceship, they will look the same as when they boarded. From their point of view, they were only away for a couple of hours, but from ours, it would have been 20 years later.

The only difference between time and eternity
is the level of energy that exists between the two.

Therefore, we must understand there is an eternal or spiritual realm/world, also referred to as: the "eternal present." To better understand the concept of time, let us trace an imaginary line. This line has a beginning and an end. Now, trace an imaginary circle. A circle has no beginning and no end. Eternity is the same as a circle, without a beginning or an end. When we enter eternity, things "are"; with no beginning or end.

God's natural habitat is eternity. When we enter the eternal dimension where faith operates, we are, in fact, crossing over the line of *time* into *eternity*.

Events of great importance took place in the *eternal* and *temporal* worlds. For instance, the event at the cross took place in the eternal realm, before the foundation of the world, when time did not yet exist. Jesus said, "I AM" prior to Abraham's existence—

speaking in terms of His eternal nature or eternal present. Additionally, since Jesus' crucifixion occurred in a particular time in history, (over two thousand years ago), His sacrifice is valid in both realms. Once Jesus was crucified at the cross and was raised from the dead, He entered the eternal realm and filled all of eternity, making His blood ageless due to its eternal nature.

We see this principle take place with Abraham. He entered eternity's timeline two thousand years prior to the crucifixion, where he was able to embrace the power of the cross and be saved by the eternal blood of Jesus. He also had communion with Melchizedek—Jesus—the High Priest of the New Testament, to whom he gave his tithes and offerings and with whom he also celebrated the Lord's Supper with bread and wine. On this occasion, animals were not sacrificed because Abraham did not have to fulfill any requirements of the law; he simply lived in the grace of the New Covenant—two thousand years before the event actually took place in time. This was made possible because once he entered the spiritual realm, Abraham was able to enjoy the benefits that God had given him in eternity.

"¹For this Melchizedek, king of Salem, priest of the Most High God, who met Abraham returning from the slaughter of the kings and blessed him, ²to whom also Abraham gave a tenth part of all, first being translated "king of righteousness," and then also king of Salem, meaning "king of peace". Hebrews 7.1, 2

A thousand years later, David had a revelation of the cross and did the same as Abraham (Psalms 22). He raised a tabernacle where he could enter the presence of God without the obstacle of a veil. According to the law, anyone who tried doing that would fall to his death, instantly. However, David was living under New Testament times and conditions: under grace, where the believers worshipped God behind the veil—in the Holy of Holies—where they could see His glory, firsthand. David was a man living in Old Testament times, but as a New Testament believer—in complete intimacy with the Father. This took place about one thousand years before the veil was completely (from top to bottom) ripped at the time of Jesus' death. The rupture of the veil was an eternal event that *also* took place in the temporal realm.

You must choose whether to live in the realm of time or eternity. If we begin to live in the eternal realm, today, we will also begin to receive all its benefits while still living on Earth, today. In eternity, we can move and operate through faith, by which all things are possible.

"18...while we do not look at the things which are seen, but at the things which are not seen. For the things which are seen are temporary, but the things which are not seen are eternal." 2 Corinthians 4.18

We must be delivered from living according to our five natural senses. Faith is not limited by any of those limitations; it does not have to understand, feel, touch, or see—it only needs to know that it "is." We receive our miracle through exercising our faith and by confessing and knowing that what we expect to receive already "is."

What trap did the kingdom of darkness set up to make us fall?

The enemy makes us believe that time is our limitation; for instance, the financial world created the thirty year system in which we can pay off our home, but when we finish paying for it, it will have cost three times more than its original price. The time established by the financial entity restricts and determines the way we pay off our mortgage loan, but what would happen if we rebel against that system and take a different approach to the system in place? What if we decide, by faith, to pay off our mortgage loan in ten years instead of thirty? It can be done because we live in a superior Kingdom where its laws are superior to human laws.

Illustration: An individual visits his doctor who tells him the bad news that he has cancer and only has three months to live;

this is the prognosis given in the natural, but there is a Kingdom that operates with superior laws which are above the natural laws of medicine. If that same individual enters the Kingdom, by faith, he will be instantly healed. In the Kingdom of God, there is no sickness because it is illegal. Sickness has no legal right to operate in the Kingdom of God.

---

*Time is a measure that keeps man from entering eternity,
but Jesus destroyed the limitations set by time
and taught us to take hold of eternal life.*

We must change our mentality. We are no longer subject to the laws of this satanic and manmade system. Therefore, we can no longer allow the enemy to limit us with time. We must live as citizens of a supernatural Kingdom in which there is an overabundance of peace, joy, health, and blessings. Through faith, we can enter eternity at any time because faith is not limited by time. As David and Abraham did before us, we can live the blessings that were limited to be ours ten, twenty, or a hundred years from now, today!

How do we cross over from being Earthly believers to becoming believers of the supernatural Kingdom?

❖ Earthy believers believe in God but live enslaved by the natural and human laws that restrict this world. They have no power to change their circumstance and the enemy does what he pleases with them; their only hope lies in going to heaven to be with Jesus after their death, but while they are still on Earth, they settle for defeated and powerless lives.

Throughout history, we see there is a fine line that separates God's people from those who still wait for the arrival of their Messiah and His Kingdom and from those who received Jesus and His Kingdom. Accordingly, the prophet, John the Baptist, announced the coming of Jesus and His Kingdom, he prepared the way for Jesus, he spoke the language of the

Kingdom, and he taught the right doctrine. However, he did not establish the government of God because he never did what was needed to make it manifest. He did not perform any sings, wonders, or miracles; he simply talked about the Kingdom but failed to add the essential ingredient: supernatural power.

"⁴¹Then many came to Him and said, "John performed no sign, but all the things that John spoke about this Man were true." John 10.41

John did not live by faith and neither did he perform any works by faith. We can say the same of millions of believers around the world today. They speak the right words, have the right doctrine, but live without power. They do nothing to make the Kingdom come. They do not heal the sick or rebuke demons. John the Baptist was killed by Herod because he lacked the power to defeat the spiritual principalities and strongholds that operated in those days.

❖ Kingdom believers continue the ministry that Jesus established on Earth by doing the same, and more, of what He did.

"¹²Most assuredly, I say to you, he who believes in Me, the works that I do he will do also; and greater works than these he will do, because I go to My Father." John 14.12

This type of believer has crossed the line: from merely pretty and/or eloquent words to a live demonstration of a resurrected Jesus with a Kingdom far more powerful than any other. Are you willing to cross over and go from being an earthly believer to a Kingdom believer?

John the Baptist was eliminated by the satanic powers of his time because he did not walk in the power of the Kingdom (Elijah experienced the same in the Old Testament). As a matter of fact, there was a moment in John the Baptist's life when he doubted Jesus, even after he declared Jesus to be the Messiah and found himself to be unworthy of loosening His sandal strap. When Jesus heard his doubt, He used the fruit of power the gospel of the Kingdom bares, as a reply.

"¹Now it came to pass, when Jesus finished commanding His twelve disciples, that He departed from there to teach and to preach in their cities. ²And when John had heard in prison about the works of Christ, he sent two of[a] his disciples ³and said to Him, "Are You the Coming One, or do we look for another?" ⁴Jesus answered and said to them, "Go and tell John the things which you hear and see: ⁵The blind see and the lame walk; the lepers are cleansed and the deaf hear; the dead are raised up and the poor have the gospel preached to them." Matthew 11.1-5

In these verses, Jesus declared the visible manifestation of God's Kingdom—the supernatural, powerful, and superior Kingdom—a Kingdom of words *and* power.

Jesus is the Same Yesterday, Today, and Forever

"⁸Jesus Christ is the same yesterday, today, and forever."
Hebrews 13.8

Jesus has not changed and will never change. On the contrary, we are the ones who need to change. We have the power and authority to perform the same works that Jesus did, but in order for this to occur, we must begin to believe and act upon the power we were given by the Holy Spirit.

Jesus was Raised from the Dead and Now Lives

"³...to whom He also presented Himself alive after His suffering by many infallible proofs, being seen by them during forty days and speaking of the things pertaining to the kingdom of God." Acts 1.3

168 | The Kingdom of God and Its Righteousness

Many will not believe simply by listening. We must show them the works of the Kingdom which include: healing, miracles, signs, wonders, and the casting out of demons. Why do we limit ourselves to demonstrating only part of the Kingdom? Why should we experience only part of what the Kingdom has for us, if it is so rich, extensive, infinite, and above all, powerful enough to change what natural laws or resources could never change? The supernatural Kingdom of God will manifest in the lives of those who choose to cross the line and go from words into actions—from good teachings into powerful demonstrations.

An unbeliever's faith can only be awakened
by supernatural works, not by pretty words.

Chapter 8

THE MYSTERIES OF THE KINGDOM

W hen we read the Word, we discover it is full of mysteries; for instance, the mystery of Christ, the mystery of the Holy Trinity, the mystery of the antichrist, and the mysteries of the Kingdom. All of creation is full of incomprehensible mysteries which our human mind cannot fathom and can only be understood through revelation, given by the Holy Spirit.

It is the desire of God's heart to fully reveal the mysteries of the Kingdom to mankind. He wants everyone to understand and obey them, and become genuine disciples of the Kingdom. God hides His mysteries only from those who want to acquire knowledge without relationship. Many want the mysteries of God unveiled but only so they can fill their minds with knowledge yet with no intention of obeying. God does not work this way. The mysteries of the Kingdom belong to His obedient children.

What is a mystery? If we look for the word *mystery* in the original Greek writings of the New Testament, we find it is the word *musterion* which signifies something that goes beyond the possibility of being known through natural channels. It can only be received through divine revelation from the Holy Spirit, in a way and time specifically appointed by God, and only to those who hunger and thirst to know Him and who willingly obey Him.

In broad terms, the word *mystery* is withheld knowledge; not because God wants to keep it hidden but because it is reserved for those with the right intentions. A divine mystery is not kept hidden from those who genuinely wish to obey by putting it to practice because it is meant to be revealed and declared precisely for that reason. In other words, it is knowledge available but held back from those who stand outside of the Kingdom.

What is divine revelation? The term *revelation* comes from the Greek verb *apokalyptō* which means: to uncover or lay open what was veiled or covered up; to disclose, to make bare, to make known, to make manifest, or to disclose what was unknown to the natural eye or to the natural ear by the Holy Spirit, to our spirit.

These divine truths are found in Scripture and have been revealed, declared, uncovered, and made known to all of us who genuinely desire to know them and obey them. In the spiritual realm, these truths were revealed, decoded and are no longer a secret. The only prerequisite to grasping these truths is to stop depending on our human mind because the only way to access these mysteries is through the Holy Spirit.

As established in the previous paragraph, God already revealed these mysteries through the Holy Spirit.

"⁹But as it is written: "Eye has not seen, nor ear heard, nor have entered into the heart of man the things which God has prepared for those who love Him." ¹⁰But God has revealed them to us through His Spirit. For the Spirit searches all things, yes, the deep things of God."
1 Corinthians 2.9, 10

These mysteries are found in the Word of God but no one can access them by natural or human means. Traditions, old mental paradigms, and stubborn hearts, will blind or cloud our understanding. To have free access to the mysteries in the Word, we need to have an open mind that is completely free of prejudice, mental, and religious strongholds.

To access the mysteries in the Bible,
we need to have an open mind,
free from prejudice and religious strongholds.

Divine mysteries were already revealed by the Holy Spirit; they were already decoded. Therefore, there are no obstacles standing in the way of those who genuinely yearn to know and obey God.

At this point, it is important to note that scripture mentions mysteries and revealed secrets, but it also mentions the *secret things* of God. The latter, by God's sovereign choice, are *yet* to be revealed.

What are the *secret things*?

The *secret things* are hidden and classified matters to which no one has access, except God.

"²⁹The secret things belong to the LORD our God, but those things which are revealed belong to us and to our children forever, that we may do all the words of this law." Deuteronomy 29.29

The difference between mysteries and *secret things* is that mysteries are declassified and decoded truths that at some point were *secret things;* but now, they are revealed through the Holy Spirit. On the other hand, *secret things* have yet to be revealed and no one, except God, has access to them. Jesus declared that the church would be edified once they received revelation of who He is; correspondently, the mysteries of God are revealed to enlighten or edify the church. As a result, He chose the apostles and prophets as administrators of these mysteries, leaving the *secret things* only to the omniscience of God.

"¹Let a man so consider us, as servants of Christ and stewards of the mysteries of God." 1 Corinthians 4.1

The Greek word for *stewards* is *oikonomos* which means: the manager of a household or of household affairs; it also means: supervisor, treasurer, preacher of the gospel, or administrator. This is the role or function of the apostle. The apostle's ministry is a governmental gift, within the church, that has God's delegated authority to distribute, supervise, and preach divine mysteries in a way that edifies the body of Christ.

When the church fails to recognize the ministerial function of an apostle as the administrator of the mysteries of God, it risks being misled by false doctrines which inevitably lead to heresy and apostasy.

Accordingly, apostles have the authority to establish if a revelation or doctrine comes from God or not, because they are the stewards, administrators, supervisors, and treasurers of the mysteries of God, including the grace of God, His people, and natural goods. Also, they are responsible for distributing these things to the church and for establishing the apostolic doctrine so it can be edified through divine revelation.

It is important to note that these mysteries are never taken outside the parameters established by the Word. If that were to happen, they would eventually become a heresy or a strange doctrine. For this reason, the apostles of the Kingdom should preach these mysteries with wisdom and love, with the intention to build up the church and establish its foundation on the Truth.

"⁵... which in other ages was not made known to the sons of men, as it has now been revealed by the Spirit to His holy apostles and prophets..." *Ephesians 3.5*

Additionally, it is very important to keep in mind that, although apostles are the administrators of these mysteries, they are not the only ones who have access to them. Rather, the access to the mysteries of God and the Kingdom are reserved for every individual who genuinely and wholeheartedly desires to know and obey them.

How did Jesus teach the mysteries of the Kingdom?

Jesus taught the mysteries of the Kingdom through parables.

What is a parable?

A *parable* is the Hebrew word *mashal* which means: proverb, proverbial saying, aphorism, byword, similitude, poem, sentences of ethical wisdom, or ethical maxims. It defines the unknown by using what is known, and entices the audience to unveil the hidden message. Parables are illustrations that reveal the truth of God in figurative language designed to touch the heart via the imagination; these are simple picturesque illustrations that challenge the mind through everyday story-telling.

Why did Jesus teach in parables?

Jesus used parables in His teachings to illustrate the message of the Kingdom; an example of a parable can be found in the book of Mark, chapter 4—the Parable of the Sower.

"¹³And He said to them, "Do you not understand this parable? How then will you understand all the parables?" Mark 4.13

Parables taught by Jesus
were intended to penetrate our hearts
and change our lives forever.

It is extremely important for people to understand that parables were used in order to interpret the Scripture correctly. See what Matthew has to say about this:

"¹⁹Whoever therefore breaks one of the least of these commandments, and teaches men so, shall be called least in the Kingdom of heaven; but whoever does and teaches them, he shall be called great in the Kingdom of heaven." Matthew 5.19

The mystery enclosed in this particular Scripture is that all those who interpret the Word correctly will be called "great in the Kingdom;" moreover, if the interpretation is given by the Holy Spirit, it will have the power to change and improve mankind. On the other hand, if the revelation is misinterpreted, it will be powerless; unable to transform lives. This further confirms the importance of having and executing the ministry of an apostle.

If we partially interpret Scripture, then the supernatural power of the Kingdom will also partially manifest. Respectively, if we misinterpret, there will be no manifestation. And if we interpret accurately, we witness the full supernatural power of the Kingdom's operations.

Why were parables used?

- To illustrate the teachings of the Kingdom of God in a way that facilitates understanding and remembering the message.

- To challenge the listener into becoming a disciple of the Kingdom of God.

- To hide certain divine virtues from those who do not wish to obey them.

The will of the Lord was to teach the Kingdom's mysteries and illustrate them through parables that make it easier for the world to understand and subsequently choose to become Kingdom disciples. Jesus wanted everyone to understand the message of the Kingdom and Its righteousness. Therefore, when He spoke to the disciples of the Kingdom, He said the following:

"¹¹Because it has been given to you to know the mysteries of the Kingdom of heaven, but to them it has not been given." Matthew 13.11

On the other hand, Jesus hid these mysteries in parables to protect them from people who did not care for them. Sadly, there are people who neither care to discover these resealed mysteries of the Kingdom of God nor are they willing to obey them, even if these truths possess the power to change their destiny. This is the reason why Jesus hid the truth behind beautiful, picturesque stories called *parables*.

"¹¹He answered and said to them, "Because it has been given to you to know the mysteries of the Kingdom of heaven, <u>but to them it has not been given.</u>" Matthew 13.11

"¹¹And He said to them, "<u>To you</u> it has been given to know the mystery of the Kingdom of God; but <u>to those who are outside</u>, all things come in parables..." Mark 4.11

"¹⁰And He said, "To you it has been given to know the mysteries of the Kingdom of God, but <u>to the rest</u> it is given in parables, that 'Seeing they may not see, and hearing they may not understand." Luke 8.10

When Jesus mentioned the word "them," He was referring to those who rejected the mysteries of the Kingdom—"they" were the religious entities of that time. When He mentioned "to you", He was referring to His disciples—those who genuinely wanted to understand and obey the mysteries of the Kingdom.

Jesus' stories were neither threatening nor imposing on people's right to choose. He simply decided to hide the truth in parables as He accomplished His mission to communicate the truth of the Kingdom and protect its integrity and righteousness. Therefore, anyone who wants to hear and obey the truth will understand it, but those who do not care for the truth, will merely hear a story.

"14 And in them the prophecy of Isaiah is fulfilled, which says: 'Hearing you will hear and shall not understand, and seeing you will see and not perceive." Matthew 13.14

Parables were meant to be understood only when truly desired. Parables are like seeds planted in a man's heart, when the time is right, if the individual wants to discover the truth, the parable will suddenly become more than a story; it will flourish to real life, as it grows, he finally understands it.

The Bible explains this event by using the expression, *when he came to himself,* which actually means that the understanding of the individual is enlightened and he is finally able to see what was right there, in front of him, all along. Often, we want to help or guide others wi-thout, first, having the truth revealed in our lives. In other words, we want to help others without realizing that we are the first that need help. Remember, one blind person cannot guide another blind person. The prodigal son *came to himself.* He realized how absurd his situation was and how immature and irresponsible he had been in caring for his inheritance. When he finally recognized the error in his ways and understood that he needed help, God revealed in his heart the knowledge that had been kept from him.

We have great knowledge stored in our hearts,
but we must be willing to obey it for it to be revealed.

Jesus spoke plain and clear to His disciples, but to the rest, He spoke in parables. He did so, to hide the mysteries of the Kingdom from those who did not care for them. Today, many hear the Word but fail to understand it and obey it, thus, causing their hearts to harden over time. Most people spend a great deal of time studying theology, but as much as they learn, they are still totally ignorant and in the dark about God; not because they lack the intellect or study skills to accomplish it, but rather, because God hides those mysteries due to their arrogance and pride.

Thus far, we can conclude that most people have information about God and the Bible, but they have yet to receive the revelation of the mysteries of the Kingdom. A person without revelation and feeding only on other's recycled information, will live without a sense of purpose or direction, going through life feeling sad, bitter, and empty. They have failed to establish a close and intimate relationship with God and have refused to seek the truth and receive the mysteries of the Kingdom—their lives will continue the same path unless they repent and seek Him wholeheartedly.

Jesus Called the Mysteries of the Kingdom, *Pearls*

"Do not give what is holy to the dogs; nor cast your pearls before swine, lest they trample them under their feet, and turn and tear you in pieces." Matthew 7.6

Jesus taught the mysteries of the Kingdom through parables, like the one just mentioned in the preceding verse. There, He refers to the revelations of the Kingdom's mysteries as *pearls*. With this declaration, He stated two important things: first, we are not to give the holy or sacred things of God to the dogs; and second, we are not to waste the revelation on swine.

"Do not give what is holy to the dogs ..."

In this verse, dogs is a metaphor for people who choose to live without Christ and practice a sinful lifestyle—doing that which is immoral before the eyes of God. They have no desire to receive the sacred or holy things of God because their desires and appetites target illicit sex, fame, religion, a position in society, love of money, wealth, or other areas too many to mention. They have no desire to discover or understand the mysteries of the Kingdom; hence, Jesus said we should not throw what is holy or sacred to this type of person. Dogs, is also a metaphor for people who stand in the background waiting for an opportunity to destroy you if and when you are not in agreement with their doctrine or mentality. They are the Pharisees, the religious "Christians;" the hypocrites who try to earn their salvation by doing works of the flesh.

"...nor cast your pearls before swine ..."

Swine is a metaphor that represents the men and women who do not value God or the divine mysteries of the Kingdom. They are compared to swine because they, too, love to dwell in the filthiness of sin. If given the opportunity to cleanse themselves in clean fresh water, regardless of efforts made to keep them clean and perfumed, they still prefer the mud and filth, over cleanliness. These types of persons do not understand the value of the mysteries, the Word, or the revelation of God.

Our society is full of swine; people who do not value their spouses, families, business, or their relationship with God. They exchange what is good and pure for a moment of pleasure, which ultimately leads them to the filthy mud as they destroy their families, lives, and goods. Jesus recommends that we not share the *pearls* or revelations of His mysteries to individuals who do not care to receive them because once they realize the revelations are beyond their understanding, they will step all over them.

The Parable of the Sower

When Jesus shared the parable of the sower, He did it to teach us the mystery of how to receive and understand the revelations. As He shared it, He illustrated the four types of listeners of the Word or the four types of ground on which the seed of the gospel might be planted.

The seed is the Word of God and the sower is Jesus or a preacher of the gospel. The four types of ground are the different types of hearts into which the Word will be planted: rocky, with thorns, by the side of the road, and good ground. As we learn this, we will also discover the four types of disciples we can find in the Kingdom.

In a farm, the ground's condition determines the seed's growth and the success or failure of its harvest. Furthermore, it is important to understand the productivity of the seed has little to do with whom the sower is but much to do with the type of ground on which it is planted.

During the time that Jesus was on Earth, Jewish life centered on learning the Word of the Lord with the goal of becoming teachers and make disciples. Every teacher had disciples because that was their teaching method. Similarly, Jesus calls men to be His disciples, but He waits for them to make the choice of following Him. Being a disciple is a calling not an obligation.

What are the four types of listeners and Kingdom disciples?

1. People who do not understand the Word and reject it.

"19When anyone hears the word of the kingdom, and does not understand it, then the wicked one comes and snatches away what was sown in his heart. This is he who received seed by the wayside."
Matthew 13.19

This type of person hears the Word but rejects it because he does not understand it. In this case, it is easy for the evil one to immediately steal the revelation because the philosophies, beliefs, and traditions practiced by them are obstacles to receiving the Word of God. Others may not be able to see the truth of the Kingdom, which can deliver them from darkness, because of

THE MYSTERIES OF THE KINGDOM | 181

their pain, rejection, or suffering. Their sad condition makes it easy for Satan to steal the seed.

2. People who joyfully receive the Word but quickly stumble and fall.

"20But he who received the seed on stony places, this is he who hears the word and immediately receives it with joy; 21yet he has no root in himself, but endures only for a while. For when tribulation or persecution arises because of the word, immediately he stumbles."
Matthew 13.20, 21

It is difficult for some people to realize the implications of entering the Kingdom. Consequently, when they begin to experience the enemy's attacks or when complications rise, they would rather walk away instead of confronting the problems. Their inability to handle and face the situations that might arise causes them to stumble and fail; thus, the Word never has a chance to take root and prosper in their hearts.

People who want to live an easy
and trouble-free gospel will, sooner or later,
stumble over the rock of commitment.

---

3. People who allow the seed to be choked and become unfruitful.

"22Now he who received seed among the thorns is he who hears the word, and the cares of this world and the deceitfulness of riches choke the word, and he becomes unfruitful." Matthew 13.22

In this verse and in others, Jesus teaches that there are three things that choke the seed or the Word of the Kingdom: the worries of this world, deceitfulness of wealth, and coveting. I know of people who received Jesus as their Lord and Savior; they surrendered their hearts to Him, made Him their Lord, and started to establish a close and intimate relationship with Him. Their love and passion for God led them to serve Him. However, after a time, they got involved in business ventures, sports, careers, and other areas of their lives, and in doing so, they placed God in second place. When the worries and passions of life took God's place, they eventually walked away from the church, stopped reading the Bible, and the life of the Word was choked and died. Today, they are separated and no longer walking with God because their seed did not bear lasting fruit.

4. People who hear the Word and accepted it.

"²³But he who received seed on the good ground is he who hears the word and understands it, who indeed bears fruit and produces: some a hundredfold, some sixty, some thirty." Matthew 13.23

The fourth type of listener is the one who receives the Word, believes it, practices what he hears, and bears long-lasting fruit. However, within this type, there are different levels of productivity or harvest. The seed was planted, it grew, and bore fruit; however, the amount of fruit varies, some will bear more than others. Likewise, there are disciples who receive the Word, believe it, grow, mature, and bear fruit at different rates—*some a hundredfold, some sixty, some thirty.* Now, let us briefly review the pre-requisites to bearing fruit:

- **Hear** the Word with spiritual ears, not just carnal ears.

- **Understand** the Word in the Spirit. Otherwise, the devil will have an easy time stealing it away.

- **Receive** the Word. When an individual hears the Word, understands it, and receives Jesus as Lord and Savior, the seed—the Word which is Jesus—begins to bear fruit.

- **Obey** the Word. To obey is to decide to become a Kingdom disciple without taking into account how much money, rejection, criticism, or segregation that decision represents.

- **Persevere** in the Word. At this level, the fruit multiplies a hundred-fold. Once the Word of God is heard and the mysteries are revealed, we can make the decision of becoming a disciple of the Kingdom of God and of Jesus. Subsequently, we persevere to obey those truths. Lastly, we are able to bear fruit at a hundred-fold level.

What conditions does God expect us to meet in order to receive revelation of the Kingdom's mysteries?

❖ To hunger and thirst for them.
❖ To be humble and be teachable.
❖ To obey the truths and revelations given by the Holy Spirit.

"25At that time Jesus answered and said, "I thank You, Father, Lord of heaven and Earth, that You have hidden these things from the wise and prudent and have revealed them to babes."
Matthew 11.25

For instance, it is impossible for someone who is experiencing marital difficulty not to consider the possibility of divorce, but if that someone is a disciple of the Kingdom, he will fight to the end to uphold his marriage covenant because he values the Word; therefore, he will reject (not even contemplate the idea) divorce. In other words, he will not disobey God.

Those who do not value what they hear and receive, will lose even that which was given to them.

"25For whoever has, to him more will be given; but whoever does not have, even what he has will be taken away from him."
Mark 4.25

The level of revelation we receive, depends on the level that we value the Word. In other words, the more we value what we receive, the more we receive. Likewise, the less we value it, the less we receive and even that which we receive will be taken away.

Illustration: There was a certain group of men who walked with God, had a close relationship with Him, and even heard His voice. One day, however, they disobeyed a mandate and hid specific truths and mysteries given by the Lord for the purpose of edifying His people; while others took the revelations given by the Holy Spirit to them, and other men of God, very lightly. In light of their attitude, they failed to live in integrity and surrendered to lies and false doctrines. A spirit of deceit took over and began to operate in their lives; not only did it stop their blessings but what they had was also taken away.

Some believe that because God has taken them to great levels of glory and success, they are exempt from fully obeying the voice of the Holy Spirit or the revealed Word of God, but they are sadly mistaken. No one is exempt; everyone must obey. It does not matter if they are apostles, prophets, doctors, lawyers, farmers, housewives, presidents of a nation, senators, congressmen, young, old, man, or woman, everyone *must* obey the Word of God. We are all subject to the government of the Kingdom of God; inherently, complete obedience is a must. Jesus ordained that His church be built on the revelation of His Word and on the mysteries of the Kingdom, not on information provided by man or birthed through inspiration of men.

In conclusion, God wants to reveal His mysteries to all, but hides them from those who do not care to obey them. These individuals can see but do not really see. They can hear but do not understand. No one can see and understand unless they decide to value and obey the revelations needed to become a Kingdom disciple. People who choose not to value what they hear about the Kingdom of God, even what they have, will be taken away.

Jesus received complete revelation of the divine mysteries because of His passion to obey and please the Father.

Chapter 9

THE GOSPEL OF THE KINGDOM

J esus began His ministry on Earth by preaching the gospel of the Kingdom. He proclaimed His principal mission: To announce the Kingdom and the good news.

"[14]Now after John was put in prison, Jesus came to Galilee, preaching the gospel of the Kingdom of God, [15]and saying, "The time is fulfilled, and the Kingdom of God is at hand. Repent, and believe in the gospel."
Mark 1.14, 15

❖ The time is fulfilled

Today is the right time to establish the Kingdom of God throughout the Earth; this is the time which He promised to us thousands of years ago. It is the designated time for the Kingdom of God, its righteousness, joy, and peace to be established among us. When Jesus speaks of time, He is actually making emphasis on the urgency of preaching His message. Now, is the time for man to, once again, be under the governing umbrella of God; this is the heart and the main goal of the gospel.

The time has come for all of mankind to draw close
and be under the covering of God's government.
This is the heart of the gospel.

❖ The Kingdom of God is at hand

Jesus announced that no man, since Adam until John the Baptist, had spoken on the Kingdom. However, with Him, the government of God was at hand and was now among men, and His mission was to announce it and establish it.

How does one understand and receive the Kingdom?

❖ Repentance

Let us make note of a very meaningful statement made by Jesus. He was not inviting people to receive forgiveness for their sins, but rather, He was telling them to repent. The reason for this was because for one to enter the Kingdom, one must first repent of one's sins. To be born again is not as simple as making the decision to believe in Jesus or the desire to have our sins forgiven. No! That is not what Jesus said. In fact, the forgiveness of our sins is the result of *genuine repentance.*

What is the definition of genuine repentance?

True repentance involves a complete change of heart and a complete turnaround in the way we think and live; it is when we desire to change because we finally realize how damaging being in charge of our own lives and decisions can be. It may sound paradoxical, right? Especially when we consider our society's idiosyncrasy as it teaches the complete opposite: "Freedom can only be found when we are able to control our lives, according to our personal criteria and understanding." Nonetheless, it is clear that man's ability to govern himself is ineffective. Otherwise, there would be no need for endless laws, trying to restrict human behavior; and neither would such laws be transgressed by the same people that create them or who are supposed to observe them.

Many of us really do want to improve the way we live, but in doing so, we are unwilling to surrender all control to God. Keep in mind this has nothing to do with surrendering control of our lives to just *anyone*. We are talking about surrendering to the *only* One who has the sovereignty and omniscience to truly know what is best for us, according to the purpose for which He created us. Jesus said, "Repent! Change the way you think, stop trying to govern yourselves, and surrender your lives to me. Stop making decisions and taking action without me; depend on me once more and your lives will completely change." Jesus asked this of us, precisely because He wants to give us a *better* life.

❖ **Believe in the gospel**

The word *gospel*, in Greek, is the word *euaggeliongo euaggelizō*, and it means: to announce the good news; good news from God.

According to Scripture, we should repent and believe the good news of the gospel, and through repentance, enter the Kingdom of God. Now, if forgiveness follows repentance, and we genuinely repent, then forgiveness is guaranteed; but remember, entering the Kingdom must come first.

People's lives change completely when they willingly surrender the control of their lives to God. No one can improve their quality of life or become better by their own strength; this is what religious people do: They try to change the methods, norms, traditions, and laws, but in doing so, either nothing changes or they make a bad situation worse. In order to fully surrender our lives to the government of God, we must *believe* and *trust* that the gospel is good. It is easy to say the Kingdom has come to us, but has it really come? Who is governing your life, you or God?

My testimony: Twenty years ago, I surrendered my life to the Lord. From then on, it has been a very difficult journey to get me to where I am today. Since I was trying to accomplish things in my own strength, there were times when I simply wanted to *throw in the towel* because I was unsure I would be able to do all that was expected of me. However, when I surrendered the control of my life to the Lord, I realized it was the best decision to make because it set me free! Now, I was able to enjoy life and feel good. I made the best decision: To *believe* the good news of the Kingdom and completely *rely* on God.

What is the good news of the Kingdom? News can be easily considered "good;" for instance, the news that you will be given a free house or that you will be getting a promotion at work. In fact, many religions teach that believing in their doctrines and ideals will produce good or peace in your life. But the good news of the Kingdom of God is incomparably different and is completely unrelated to religion.

"14And this gospel of the Kingdom will be preached in all the world as a witness to all the nations, and then the end will come." Matthew 24.14

The good news of the Kingdom has two parts:

1. Mankind and the government of God were restored. As a result of repentance, obedience, and observing divine justice through faith.

2. The message of the cross: Announcing Jesus as the One crucified and raised from the dead a conqueror, with power and authority.

Man's restoration to the lordship of God
and the message of the cross is the good news
transforming our society.

Both parts, make up the good news of the Kingdom, and are components that distinguish the Kingdom's gospel against others. Both, revolutionized society in those days, throughout days of the first apostles, and continue to do so throughout the ages—changing the lives of every believer. In other words, the same gospel introduced by Jesus, is still causing the same revolutionizing effect every time it is preached, proclaimed, announced, and taught with its two ingredients. It is pertinent for the good news of the Kingdom to be announced in its entirety; that is, with both parts always announced, together. If one part is taught without the other, the gospel becomes fickle and powerless. Today, many (ministers and godly men and women) preach a partial version of the gospel but not the complete true gospel of the Kingdom; they are settling for a gospel that does not change lives. The power to transform and alter the course of our lives by leading us away from devastation and perdition into salvation and a life full of blessings, is the intrinsic result of only one gospel: the one first brought to us by Jesus—in its entirety.

As previously stated, the gospel of the Kingdom is what Satan fears most. Ironically, this is the reason Satan shows up wherever the gospel is preached: to try and steal it from the minds of the people who hear it.

"¹⁸Therefore hear the parable of the sower: ¹⁹When anyone hears the word of the Kingdom, and does not understand it, then the wicked one comes and snatches away what was sown in his heart. This is he who received seed by the wayside." Matthew 13.18, 19

Thousands of believers give their tithes and offerings in support of ministries "spreading the good news of the gospel to the ends of the Earth." Sadly, and unknowingly, many are really only financing a different gospel than the one Jesus taught. This could be the result of one of two things: one, ministers and ministries target their messages to please the audience instead of pleasing God; or, two, although they have a pure heart for God, they have limited knowledge in their sincere effort to extend the Kingdom. Let us see what the apostle Paul said about this:

"⁹As we have said before, so now I say again, if anyone preaches any other gospel to you than what you have received, let him be accursed. ¹⁰For do I now persuade men, or God? Or do I seek to please men? For if I still pleased men, I would not be a bondservant of Christ." Galatians 1.9, 10

Why are some of us not preaching the gospel of the Kingdom?

The choice of leaving everything behind to answer the call of preaching and planting the seed of the Kingdom's gospel is a very rewarding experience; however, it is also one that brings much persecution. For the most part, people are not eager to experience persecution for the gospel's sake. Their choice to avoid such confrontation motivates them to preach a less controversial message, one that lines up according to the society they are trying to please. However, if their point of view was in line with the Kingdom of God, that alone, would modify their personal life and compel them to exhaust every avenue that keeps them from compromising Kingdom principles. The outcome would be a lifestyle that reflects the life of Christ.

If we preach the gospel of the Kingdom, then we will have a mindset or point of view from the Kingdom. An ordinary gospel cannot be compared to the gospel of the Kingdom; a Kingdom church cannot be compared to just any church; a Kingdom family cannot be compared to just any family; a Kingdom business cannot be compared to just any business; a Kingdom city cannot be compared to just any city. Preaching the true gospel is completely different from other experiences. Our families, business, and church should be different if we preach and live the pure gospel of the Kingdom. Jesus lived differently to the people around Him. The apostles lived a radically different life. Preaching the gospel of the Kingdom brings great rewards and blessings in our lives on Earth and in the one to come (in eternity).

Two things make the gospel of the Kingdom different: The restoration of man with the government of God and the message of the cross.

1. The restoration of man to the government of God.

In order to properly introduce the good news of the Kingdom, we must first recognize that the problem the world and society faces today is a matter of government. If the right government was established, the world would be at peace and enjoying justice.

In the beginning, God created man to dwell within His government. Man was dependent on God while God was the spring of life that supplied all of man's needs. Man allowed the life of God to flow through him while being entirely submitted to His authority. The moment man stepped out of that government, it created the greatest problem that mankind has ever encountered and still faces today.

"¹And you He made alive, who were dead in trespasses and sins, ²in which you once walked according to the course of this world, according to the prince of the power of the air, the spirit who now works in the sons of disobedience, ³among whom also we all once conducted ourselves

in the lusts of our flesh, fulfilling the desires of the flesh and of the mind, and were by nature children of wrath, just as the others."
Ephesians 2.1-3

If we were all to submit to the government and authority of God, every problem faced by society today would cease to exist. The heart of the gospel is to bring the solution. The worse sins committed by mankind are the direct result of their independence from God.

Jesus said, *"Come to Me, all you who labor and are heavy laden, and I will give you rest. I will give you the answer to every problem you might be facing. Enter the government of God and find rest from your burdens."*

If you are a rebellious person who chooses not to submit to the government of God, then you are in total contradiction. Why?—because if rebellion is not permitted in an Earthly kingdom, much less is it permitted in the Kingdom of God. One purpose for the gospel of the Kingdom is for man to return to a state of total obedience and submission to its governmental system.

"[16]...that I might be a minister of Jesus Christ to the Gentiles, ministering the gospel of God, that the offering of the Gentiles might be acceptable, sanctified by the Holy Spirit. [17]Therefore I have reason to glory in Christ Jesus in the things which pertain to God. [18]For I will not dare to speak of any of those things which Christ has not accomplished through me, in word and deed, to make the Gentiles obedient—"
Romans 15.16-18

Paul said that if his ministry did not produce obedience in word and action, then he was wasting his time. There is no gain when thousands receive Jesus as Savior but fail to obey and submit to the government of God. What truly counts is to see people receive Jesus *and* obey the gospel in word and action; these are the people who truly make a difference and make the ministry effective. This is exactly what we mean when we talk about extending the

Kingdom of God throughout the Earth. If lives are not transformed, then the Kingdom has not yet come.

If lives are not being transformed,
the Kingdom has not arrived
at your church, city, or nation.

The daily attitude of an individual who understood the gospel of the Kingdom is: to live in obedience to God and the laws and norms of His government. This attitude is manifested in the practical expressions of his daily living.

Illustration: When the natural laws dictate that cancer is incurable, Kingdom laws say:

"⁵But He was wounded for our transgressions, He was bruised for our iniquities; the chastisement for our peace was upon Him, and by His stripes we are healed." Isaiah 53.5

God established His Kingdom on Earth through different institutions that have the delegated authority given by King Jesus. We must submit to these authorities because they are authorized extensions on Earth, of the heavenly government—as long as obeying them does not imply violating God's Word, His values, or principles.

❖ **Earthly authorities**

All governmental authority that exists on Earth has been established by God, and we must respect and obey their norms and statutes.

"¹Let every soul be subject to the governing authorities. For there is no authority except from God, and the authorities that exist are appointed by God. ²Therefore whoever resists the authority resists the ordinance of God, and those who resist will bring judgment on themselves. ³For rulers are not a terror to good works, but to evil.

Do you want to be unafraid of the authority? Do what is good, and you will have praise from the same. ⁴For he is God's minister to you for good. But if you do evil, be afraid; for he does not bear the sword in vain; for he is God's minister, an avenger to execute wrath on him who practices evil. ⁵Therefore you must be subject, not only because of wrath but also for conscience' sake." Romans 13.1-5

❖ **Authorities in the home**

"¹Children, obey your parents in the Lord, for this is right."
Ephesians 6.1

Children must obey their parents' dominion; the wife must obey their husband's dominion, and the husband must obey Jesus' dominion.

❖ **Authorities in the church**

"¹⁷Obey those who rule over you, and be submissive, for they watch out for your souls, as those who must give account. Let them do so with joy and not with grief, for that would be unprofitable for you." Hebrews 13.17

Believers obey their pastor and church leaders—ministers and elders—because they are the spiritual authorities placed by God to help them grow and spiritually mature.

❖ **Authorities in the workplace**

We are subject to our supervisors and leaders. We show our submission to God in practical ways, including obeying the delegated authorities of His government. When we submit to authority, we get transformed because we have an encounter with divine government and authority. Consequently, we find the answer to the world's problems, which can be easily summed up under one (the root of all other problems): Mankind's independence from the government of God. This

196 THE KINGDOM OF GOD AND ITS RIGHTEOUSNESS

brings us back to the underlying message of the Kingdom's gospel: for every man to return to the government of God.

2. The message of the cross

The Apostle Paul preached in Athens for a long period of time, but he did not establish a church nor did anything powerful there because he wanted to try out his personal wisdom. Paul tried to be wise, ingenious, and intelligent without mentioning the message of the cross; hence, his words when he visited Corinth:

"²For I determined not to know anything among you except Jesus Christ and Him crucified." 1 Corinthians 2.2

Human wisdom is powerless
when it comes to changing hearts or saving lives;
only the message of the redeeming work at the cross
can transform lives—forever.

In Corinth, Paul decides not to make the same mistake he made in Athens. This time, he would not compromise the message of the cross just to look good in front of Greek intellectualism—he had learned his lesson.

"¹⁷For Christ did not send me to baptize, but to preach the gospel, not with wisdom of words, lest the cross of Christ should be made of no effect. ¹⁸For the message of the cross is foolishness to those who are perishing, but to us who are being saved it is the power of God." 1 Corinthians 1.17, 18

According to Paul's teachings, the message of the cross has a very important ingredient: the power of God. If the message is preached with human wisdom, the good news becomes vain and stops being the supernatural gospel of the Kingdom. For many, the message of the cross is craziness, offensive, and a stumbling block.

Paul encourages us to proclaim the good news. In Greek, the word for preach is *kēryssō*. This word means: to proclaim after the manner of a messenger, always with the suggestion of formality, gravity, and an authority which must be listened to and obeyed; to state publicly, in a loud voice, and even to the point of offending. Greek people loved human wisdom. Their society was the nest of intellectualism and humanism, and their culture negated everything that was supernatural. Paul fell in their trap, like many continue to do today, of wanting to please their minds more than saving their souls. However, Paul also learned his lesson and radically decided to preach only the resurrected Christ and the message of the cross because he understood first hand where the power of the Kingdom's gospel resides.

The power of the cross is divided in two:

❖ The type of death Jesus suffered
❖ The power of the resurrection

"²³...but we preach Christ crucified, to the Jews a stumbling block and to the Greeks foolishness, ²⁴but to those who are called, both Jews and Greeks, Christ the power of God and the wisdom of God."
1 Corinthians 1.23, 24

For the power to be loosened, it was not sufficient for Jesus to die. He had to die as a criminal—nailed to the cross, punished, and afflicted—precisely how it happened. Abandoned by God, He bore our sins, iniquities, and sickness at the cross. He died and was buried; but on the third day, after taking the keys of death and Hades back from Satan, He was raised from the dead. With His death, Jesus paid the wages of our sins and restored the relationship between God and man. With His resurrection, he conquered death and recovered the authority that man had lost in the Garden of Eden.

The gospel is *good news* because it announces the arrival of the Kingdom: The absolute order of God and the execution of His perfect will—on Earth as it is in heaven. Also, it is *good news* because it preaches the message of the cross: Christ died for our sins and was raised from the dead, leaving behind, in the grave and in hell, every transgression committed by mankind. Now, He sits at the right hand of the Father, in the Throne of Glory while He governs His Kingdom.

Paul preached the gospel of the Kingdom

"¹Moreover, brethren, I declare to you the gospel which I preached to you, which also you received and in which you stand, ²by which also you are saved, if you hold fast that word which I preached to you— unless you believed in vain. ³For I delivered to you first of all that which I also received: that Christ died for our sins according to the Scriptures, ⁴and that He was buried, and that He rose again the third day according to the Scriptures..." 1 Corinthians 15.1-4

This is the message of the good news of the gospel of the Kingdom which must be publicly announced and proclaimed. We must declare in public that Jesus died, was buried, and was raised from the dead to redeem us from certain eternal damnation. We no longer have to be slaves to sin or addictions. Jesus lives and reigns with power.

By taking a closer look at this mystery, we can conclude that the power of Jesus' resurrection was not just a physical miracle that took place. We know this because in the resurrection of Lazarus a physical miracle took place, but when Lazarus was raised from the dead, he was the same man that had died, and after a few years, he died again. Nothing changed for Lazarus except that God was glorified through the miracle of his resurrection. The sins and bad habits he had before his death were still there after his resurrection. His body, soul, and spirit were raised to the same status and condition.

In Jesus' resurrection, something different took place. Although His condition was worse and full of sin, more so than any other man because He took upon Himself the sins of the world, when He was raised from the dead, there was no evidence or trace of any sin left upon Him. When Jesus was raised, He left every sin behind in the grave or in the depths of hell where they belonged. In His resurrection, Jesus was raised to be seated on the Throne of Glory as a new Man. His death granted Him authority over Satan, with the legal right to cast him out and destroy his kingdom and every wicked deed he has against God's creation. Now, it becomes evident why the power of the resurrection is part of the good news of the Kingdom.

What evidence do we have that Jesus lives?

"²...until the day in which He was taken up, after He through the Holy Spirit had given commandments to the apostles whom He had chosen, ³to whom He also presented Himself alive after His suffering by many infallible proofs, being seen by them during forty days and speaking of the things pertaining to the Kingdom of God." Acts 1.2, 3

Everyone who has experienced great transformation and changes in our being has proof—the evidence that Jesus was raised from the dead and now lives. The resurrection differentiates Jesus from all other prophets or leaders of thousands of religions throughout the world. No other prophet or leader has been raised from the dead nor has the power and authority that Jesus conquered. My dearest reader, would you like to believe in the gospel of the Kingdom of God? If you choose to believe, your life will be transformed, forever.

What does the gospel of the Kingdom consist of?

The gospel of the Kingdom consists of two main elements that have the ability to impact and transform anyone's life.

- The preaching of the Word
- The demonstration of power

The gospel of the Kingdom will always carry these two elements when preaching it because they are inherently produced as we proclaim the Kingdom and the message of the cross. If we do not preach the gospel to its entirety, the power of the Kingdom will not be activated.

If we fail to preach the gospel to its entirety,
the power of the Kingdom will never be activated.

"⁵For our gospel did not come to you in word only, but also in power, and in the Holy Spirit and in much assurance, as you know what kind of men we were among you for your sake." 1 Thessalonians 1.5

The gospel is preached and taught today but only in words; therefore, hindering its positive effects—because words without power do not save, even if these are quoted from the Bible. "The demonstration of power" during or after preaching the Word, refers to the visible manifestation of God's power—healing, miracles, signs, wonders, and the expulsion of demons—that transforms lives.

In the New Testament, all churches were established on the power of signs, wonders, miracles, and the expulsion of demons. If God does not perform miracles, and if demons do not run because of you, then you are not preaching the gospel of the Kingdom, but rather, a gospel that is well spoken by using eloquent words but without power. Only the gospel of the Kingdom causes the power of God to manifest the supernatural condition of His government.

How did Paul preach in Corinth after spending three years in Athens?

"³I was with you in weakness, in fear, and in much trembling. ⁴And my speech and my preaching were not with persuasive words of human wisdom, but in demonstration of the Spirit and of power, ⁵that your faith should not be in the wisdom of men but in the power of God." 1 Corinthians 2.3-5

The Gospel of the Kingdom is More than Words; it is the Power of God

"16For I am not ashamed of the gospel of Christ, for it is the power of God to salvation for everyone who believes, for the Jew first and also for the Greek..." Romans 1.16

There is no reason to feel shame when we share the gospel because it holds the power to heal, save, deliver, and transform; it holds the power of God and the *good news* for everyone who is experiencing calamity and desperate moments.

Words and actions go hand-in-hand

"18For I will not dare to speak of any of those things which Christ has not accomplished through me, in word and deed, to make the Gentiles obedient—19in mighty signs and wonders, by the power of the Spirit of God, so that from Jerusalem and round about to Illyricum I have fully preached the gospel of Christ." Romans 15.18, 19

Once again, Paul shared the gospel of the Kingdom with words and actions. He preached in the same manner as Jesus lived, always moving in two areas: the Word and power—preaching and action.

"19And He said to them, "What things?" So they said to Him, "The things concerning Jesus of Nazareth, who was a Prophet mighty in deed and word before God and all the people..." Luke 24.19

If we proclaim a gospel with only one ingredient, it is another gospel—half the gospel. We must preach the complete gospel so the Kingdom can come, be established, and Jesus can return soon.

The good news of the Kingdom belongs to whom?

"18The Spirit of the LORD is upon Me, because He has anointed Me to preach the gospel to the poor; He has sent Me to heal the brokenhearted, to proclaim liberty to the captives and recovery of sight to the blind, to set

at liberty those who are oppressed; [19]*to proclaim the acceptable year of the* *LORD." Luke 4.18, 19*

The preceding verses correspond to Isaiah, chapter 71, found in the Old Testament. Before digging into what the Lord said in these verses, let us first discuss their background. There was a Jewish tradition stating that the first eight verses of Isaiah 71 were to be read by the Messiah when He finally arrived on Earth—no one else could read them. Therefore, everyone observed the tradition and no one dared to break it. Just imagine the thoughts and reactions of the people when Jesus started to read them. These verses read by the Son of God described the good news of the Kingdom and caused a complete and total change in mankind. Those verses contain the provision needed by all men; that is why they revolutionized the entire human race.

The gospel of the Kingdom of God:

1. Gives good news to the poor

"He has anointed Me to preach the gospel to the poor."

The first good news of the Kingdom is given to the poor. Jesus is not talking about the poor in spirit, as He did in the book of Matthew. When He refers to those who are poor, as in lack of material wealth, He simply uses the word *poor*.

Who is considered poor?

The word *poor* is the Greek word *ptōchos;* it means: reduced to extreme poverty or begging; destitute of wealth. This word suggests the last financial or social scale experienced by someone who totally lacks worldly goods.

Did you know that every time
we preach the gospel of the Kingdom
and people receive it,
material prosperity enters our territory?

Did you know that every time the gospel is preached, and people receive it, material prosperity comes to your territory?

Illustration: There is a city in Guatemala called Almolonga; this city could be considered the only city of our generation that has experienced a total spiritual and social transformation. Up to the seventies, this city was submerged in poverty, misery, licentiousness; today, it enjoys a ninety percent Christian population. The last jail was closed a few years ago because crime ceased to exist in that city. The farmers in Almolonga have prospered so much that they now sell their vegetables throughout Central America. The fruits they produce are recognized and awarded everywhere they are sold because of their excellent quality. Their products are of such high quality that a group of experts from the United States have studied them.

The gospel of the Kingdom arrived there when Pastor Mariano Risscaje started to cast out demons of alcoholism that were strongly operating in the region. In three months, he delivered, approximately, four hundred alcoholic men. After that, the revival started to take place and has continued to this day. This city has prospered to such levels that all fruits produced on that land are bigger than normal size which contributes to the high levels of exportation of their harvests. The farmers purchased trucks and machinery and developed their agriculture efforts to levels that have never been seen before in Guatemala. Today, the city of Almolonga is a flourishing city. The gospel of the Kingdom arrived with good news for the poor, transformed their lives, and led them to prosperity.

Jesus brought the *good news* to the land's disinherited; to those without material wealth, food, clothing, roof, or the essentials needed to live. The good news is that they no longer have to be poor. The gospel of the Kingdom produces abundance. That is why Jesus said:

"33But seek first the Kingdom of God and His righteousness, and all these things shall be added to you." Matthew 6.33

Why has the gospel not produced financial prosperity in other places where it is preached?

The answer is simple. People who preach it do not believe that God wants to prosper them materially; they also do not believe in the entire gospel of the Kingdom. Therefore, they preach other news. They do not understand that Jesus made Himself poor so that we could be made wealthy.

"⁹For you know the grace of our Lord Jesus Christ, that though He was rich, yet for your sakes He became poor, that you through His poverty might become rich." 2 Corinthians 8.9

If Jesus owns the world's silver and gold
and He surrendered His life for us,
what makes you think He enjoys
watching us struggle, financially?

There is no doubt that Jesus paid for our poverty, at the cross. We were redeemed by it. This is great news! Praise God!

Another gift that comes from the gospel of the Kingdom of God is:

2. It heals the brokenhearted

Who are the brokenhearted? Brokenhearted, is the Greek word *syntribō* which means: to completely crush, squash, press, to tear apart, or to break. In other words, the brokenhearted are those who are emotionally and mentally broken. Their souls are fragmented into a thousand pieces. For this reason, they have no identity, are always double-minded, and have a double personality. They experience these things due to physical, sexual, and verbal abuse; due to rejection and suffering experienced in childhood and because they have been destroyed by a cruel society that only seeks its own benefit.

*"¹The Spirit of the Lord GOD is upon Me... **He has sent Me to heal the brokenhearted**..." Isaiah 61.1*

The popular version of a Spanish Bible says, *"...to heal the fallen, the hurt, and the broken due to calamity."*

An Aramic translation says, *"...to strengthen the hurt with for-giveness."*

Our soul gets fragmented and wounded when we live contrary to the laws of the Kingdom. Many of us have lingering wounds caused by our spouses, society, and friends, and some of us are broken inside due to life itself, by failed business ventures, the death of a loved one, or by any of numerous circumstances that constantly engulf us. But take heart! God sent Jesus to bring us the *good news*, affirming us that all we need to be healed, is His divine forgiveness.

Dearest reader, what is the good news for *you*?

Divine forgiveness and inner healing is the good news that will help you pick up the pieces and start over. Jesus came to heal and take away guilt, shame, sadness, mourning, fear, inferiority com-plexes, rejection, bitterness, and condemnation. Once you were broken, but now, the good news of the Kingdom will make you whole again. You are no longer confined to your psychologists to overcome a crisis because the Kingdom of God brings profound healing to your heart. However, for this to happen, you need to believe the good news of the Kingdom. When your relationship with God's government is restored and the message of the cross penetrates your body, soul, and spirit, you will be free! Heart-broken? Receive *your* good news, today. Do not wait to finish the book to believe; believe it right now!

3. **The gospel of the Kingdom liberates the captives**

*"[18]The Spirit of the LORD is upon Me... He has sent Me to **proclaim liberty to the captives**..." Luke 4.18*

Who are the captives? *Aichmalōtos* is the Greek word for captive; it means: one that was taken captive or becomes a prisoner by force; taken by the sword. The captives are the politically and socially disinherited.

Who takes us captive?

There are three forces that imprison us: the devil, sin, and the world's system.

"26...and that they will come to their senses and escape from the trap of the devil, who has taken them captive to do his will."
2 Timothy 2.26

Millions of people are prisoners in their own homes; they are trapped by their race, ideologies, depression, pills, and/or medical treatments. They are prisoners to gambling, love of money, drugs, excessive eating, pornography, alcohol, and fear of death. They live in a cell from which they helplessly seek to escape, but repeatedly fail because the devil has them trapped in a place where there is no outlet. Are you one of the many who are being held captive by the devil and sin?

What is the good news or gospel of the Kingdom?

The good news for the captives is that they no longer have to be prisoners to the devil, the world's system, or sin. Why? Because Jesus captured captivity; in other words, the place in hell where every captive was destined to spend eternity, was overtaken by Him.

Therefore He says: 'When He ascended on high, He led captivity cap-tive, and gave gifts to men.'" Ephesians 4.8

Jesus led captivity captive, leaving it powerless—unable to exert damage against the people who receive the gospel of the King-dom and the message of the cross. Captives cannot dream even if they want to, but when they are delivered, they are free to dream. Jesus was raised from the dead, destroyed the power of captivity, and gave gifts and dreams to all men. If you feel incarcerated, receive your deliverance, right now!

"¹When the LORD brought back the captivity of Zion, we were like those who dream." Psalms 126.1

Jesus brought the good news to the captives so they could dream. When people are delivered through the power of the gospel, they are free to dream again. Free to dream of having their families restored; free to see themselves healed from depression; free to finish their studies; free to establish their own business; free to dream of helping their nation end poverty and impact their society through the power of the gospel; free to dream that their children are healed and that they have the resources to give them an education alongside the knowledge of God's unfailing love and the fear of the Lord. To be free from captivity is like having a new beginning; a new awakening or a new chance to do things right, knowing, the horrors of the past have disappeared. Now you, dear reader, are free from captivity. Receive the Kingdom's good news and dare to dream again!

———————— ❦ ————————
The ability to dream is a sign of freedom.
The more free we are, the greater the capacity to dream.
———————— ❦ ————————

The gospel of the Kingdom of God also:

4. Gives sight to the blind

"¹⁸The Spirit of the LORD is upon Me... He has sent Me to proclaim liberty to the captives and recovery of sight to the blind..."
Luke 4.18

Who are "the blind?"

The blind are not just those who are unable to see, but also those who disinherit good physical health in general and whose bodies are invaded by illness. Jesus invoked healing to our bodies at the cross—therefore, this too, is part of the good news of the Kingdom. Wherever Jesus traveled, He preached, healed, and rebuked demons. When John the Baptist doubted that Jesus was the Messiah, Jesus responded with a message that summed up the Kingdom of God and its power—His life, purpose, and ministry.

"⁴Jesus answered and said to them, "Go and tell John the things which you hear and see: ⁵The blind see and the lame walk; the lepers are cleansed and the deaf hear; the dead are raised up and the poor have the gospel preached to them." Matthew 11.4, 5

Sickness is a curse and Jesus came to redeem us from it. Therefore, we must pray for those who are sick among us: in church, the workplace, and everywhere—we, have the good news the sick are waiting to hear.

"¹³Christ has redeemed us from the curse of the law, having become a curse for us (for it is written, "Cursed is everyone who hangs on a tree..." Galatians 3.13

Jesus redeemed us from the curse of sin, sickness, and poverty. Sickness was merely a consequence of sin; however, Jesus came to deliver the good news: He paid the wages of our sin. Now, it is up to us to receive our gift of healing, today!

5. **The gospel of the Kingdom frees the oppressed**

*"The Spirit of the LORD is upon Me... He has sent Me to **set at liberty those who are oppressed**..." Luke 4.18*

Who are the oppressed?

The word *oppressed* is the Greek word *thlibō* which means: to press hard upon; in a compressed way; troubled, afflicted, or distressed. This word, metaphorically speaking, means: oppression, tension, or great anxiety; to have many loose ends and no control over any of them. Once again, we see that anguish, sadness, imprisonment, tension, and mental oppression are caused by the world, the devil, and his demons. They oppress our minds in order to successfully force us into conforming to their operational system, which inherently brings anguish and depression.

Millions live with a mental oppression that manifests itself as terrible migraine headaches. The physical pain is so intense that many would rather die than endure such terrible "head-splitting" pain. This oppression often derives from problems such as broken marriages, run-away children, financial disasters, and a loss of employment without anything to fall back on, affecting their ability to provide for their family or schooling. Everything seems to go wrong for them and many areas of their lives appear to be out of their control. They are mentally distraught, have numerous problems, and are emotionally depressed because their lives seem to be meaningless.

What is the good news of the Kingdom for the oppressed?

"38...how God anointed Jesus of Nazareth with the Holy Spirit and with power, who went about doing good and healing all who were oppressed by the devil, for God was with Him." Acts 10.38

Jesus came to heal and deliver the oppressed. With Jesus, they no longer have to live stressed out or worried about their future. Jesus conquered the world and defeated the devil and his demonic forces.

6. To proclaim "the acceptable year of the Lord"

"19To proclaim the acceptable year of the LORD." Luke 4.19

"10And you shall consecrate the fiftieth year, and proclaim liberty throughout all the land to all its inhabitants. It shall be a Jubilee for you; and each of you shall return to his possession, and each of you shall return to his family." Leviticus 25.10

What is the "acceptable year of the Lord?" This practice began in the Old Testament when the Lord gave Moses instructions on the care of the land and the harvest. The name of that practice was called *The Year of Jubilee,* and it was proclaimed every fifty years. Three things took place during that time:

- All debt was forgiven
- Every slave was set free
- All land was returned to its original owners

What is the good news? In Greek, the phrase that Jesus cried out at the cross—*"It is done!"* is *teleō* which means: to bring to a close; to finish; to end; to execute; to conclude or discharge a debt; to pay off, satisfy, end, or fulfill. In other words, there was nothing else that needed to be done because the Son of God was our *Jubilee.* "TELEO!" was a shout of victory not of pain. Jesus had triumphed; the wages of sin had been completely paid for with every drop of His blood. As a gladiator would shout to express triumph upon defeating his enemy in a Roman arena, Jesus shouted upon defeating *our* enemy.

Jesus paid the price so the captives could be set free: healed from all mental and physical infirmity; the brokenhearted healed of their emotional pain; deliver the poor and oppressed. At last, the wages of sin were forgiven, the captive were set free, and everything the devil had stolen was returned. The *acceptable year of the Lord (Jubilee)* had arrived through His death!

In those days, the good news of the Kingdom caused a revolution in society because it touched upon every area pertinent to the existence of both a single individual and society as a whole: mental, physical, spiritual, emotional, relational, financial, political, and other arenas were covered by the Kingdom's gospel.

There is only one answer
that can satisfy all mankind:
The good news of the Kingdom.

To whom did God give the gospel of the Kingdom?

After being raised from the dead, Jesus appeared to His disciples and entrusted them to spread the gospel of the Kingdom. Today, *we* are His disciples, and have also been entrusted to spread the gospel to the lost, oppressed, sick, and the captives. We must proclaim *the acceptable year of the Lord.*

"⁴But as we have been approved by God to be entrusted with the gospel, even so we speak, not as pleasing men, but God who tests our hearts." 1 Thessalonians 2.4

It is such an amazing thing that God did not entrust the gospel to the angels, but to us! What a privilege for the Lord to make us, human beings with faults and weaknesses, the carriers of the gospel of the Kingdom! However, He did not entrust us with the gospel so we can keep it hidden, but rather to preach it. The gospel of the Kingdom is the power of God, the continuation of the saving grace of Jesus Christ. Since *we* were made responsible for continuing the ministry of Jesus, we must exercise that power and establish the fullness of the Kingdom in our society. We are as He is, coheirs of the same grace.

"¹¹...according to the glorious gospel of the blessed God which was committed to my trust." 1 Timothy 1.11

Timothy was Paul's disciple, just like we are disciples of other men of God. However, the gospel is the same and it has been entrusted to every disciple in the body of Christ.

What is the mandate or commission that Jesus left the believers?

"¹⁵And He said to them, "Go into all the world and preach the gospel to every creature." Mark 16.15

* **Go**

   The word *go* illustrates the idea of traveling with the purpose of experimenting. In other words, we will not experience the power of God until we go. This mandate is for every child of the Kingdom; it is not a suggestion or a wish, it is an order that everyone must obey. We cannot just idly sit by and wait for unbelievers to arrive. That was not the mandate. The mandate was to *go!* And so we must *go!*

- **Paul said the commission was given**

"¹⁶For if I preach the gospel, I have nothing to boast of, for necessity is laid upon me; yes, woe is me if I do not preach the gospel! ¹⁷For if I do this willingly, I have a reward; but if against my will, I have been entrusted with a stewardship." 1 Corinthians 9.16, 17

Illustration: Only two percent of Christians have won a soul for Jesus, in their lives. This must change! The gospel must be preached to every adult, youth, man, woman, and child. It is not a matter of *if we want to* but a matter of *utmost necessity.*

- **We must put on the footwear and go**

"⁷How beautiful upon the mountains are the feet of him who brings good news, who proclaims peace, who brings glad tidings of good things, who proclaims salvation, who says to Zion,' Your God reigns!'" Isaiah 52.7

When we share the gospel, we wear the power of God and nothing can harm us.

Where will we go?

The mandate is to go throughout the world—to the nations, our workplaces, the cities, the towns, villages, colleges, hospitals, prisons, neighborhoods, and our own homes. We must go as Jesus went—everywhere.

"¹Now it came to pass, afterward, that He went through every city and village, preaching and bringing the glad tidings of the Kingdom of God. And the twelve were with Him." Luke 8.1

Who are we?

- ### We are witnesses of the gospel and of Jesus

"⁸But you shall receive power when the Holy Spirit has come upon you; and you shall be witnesses to Me in Jerusalem, and in all Judea and Samaria, and to the end of the Earth." Acts 1.8

A witness of Jesus is one that has undeniable evidence—firsthand experience—of the transforming power of the Kingdom of God.

A witness of Jesus has undeniable evidence;
firsthand experience of the transforming power
of the Kingdom of God.

- ### We are salt of the Earth and light of the world

"¹³You are the salt of the Earth; but if the salt loses its flavor, how shall it be seasoned? It is then good for nothing but to be thrown out and trampled underfoot by men." Matthew 5.13

Salt has three principal uses:

- It gives flavor to the food
- It is an influence that pierces and penetrates
- It preserves meats to keep them from spoiling

You can sprinkle salt on a piece of meat and the entire piece will be *influenced* by the salt. Naturally, you would not use the same amount of salt as you do meat. The salt works silently but powerfully; it works hard to avoid things from spoiling. Believers who are *salt of the Earth* keep people from choosing divorce as an option; they uphold moral values and are the salt that influences others to choose salvation. They are the people who keep everything around them preserved and unspoiled.

Jesus said, *"You are the salt of the Earth."* The potency of the Kingdom is so great that if you were to work in a building full of people, eventually, they would all be under its influence. You, as a christian, can be alone in the office or at school, surrounded by many people that do not love God; however, because you are the salt of the Earth, you must remember that the potency of the Kingdom is in your spirit. If you are convinced that God placed you where you are right now, sooner or later, every person under demonic influence will be under your influence and you will be able to establish the Kingdom in their minds and hearts. You cannot add a grain of salt on a piece of meat and not have it be affected. For that reason, you have been called to occupy difficult places. God has placed you as the salt of the Kingdom in your city, office, school, college, and everywhere you go.

Illustration: You could be in the middle of a house that is infected with drugs, homosexuality, and idolatry, but your presence there will cause people to surrender to your influence. Salt is powerful. We are affecting everything we come in contact with!

As salt adds flavor to bland foods, people search for something to add flavor into their lives. Christians are called and sent to add flavor into the lives of those who do not know Jesus.

"⁶Let your speech always be with grace, seasoned with salt, that you may know how you ought to answer each one." Colossians 4.6

The light of the world is the life of the Kingdom that lives in each believer.

"¹⁴You are the light of the world. A city that is set on a hill cannot be hidden." Matthew 5.14

Light pierces the darkness and overtakes it so everyone can see it. Salt operates in silence, but the light operates in public. The light of the believer is the credibility he has with the people that know him because it represents the good testimony he has established during his daily walk with Christ. For instance, one way to be light is to kindle a flame of vision in a church, the family, the city, and the world.

The light, a strong source of power and energy, fulfills three functions:

- It exposes or manifests the truth with revelation of the Word so we can see it and confess it.

- It eliminates darkness indefinitely.

Light and darkness cannot coexist; they are mutually exclusive; that is why Jesus was called to be the light of the world—to manifest the character of the Kingdom and influence all of humanity.

- **We are ambassadors and messengers of the Kingdom**

"20Now then, we are ambassadors for Christ, as though God were pleading through us: we implore you on Christ's behalf, be reconciled to God." 2 Corinthians 5.20

An ambassador is an individual who acts as a representative of another; he does not represent himself, and the message he transmits is never his own, but rather, it belongs to the person who trusted him with it and sent him on a diplomatic mission. In this case, Jesus is who sends us, and the mission is to preach the gospel of the Kingdom and demonstrate its power.

Illustration: An individual is sent as ambassador of the United States of America to the United Nations. Physically, he is small in stature, cross-eyed, bald, and wears thick glasses; nevertheless, people listen and respect his authority and the government he represents. We are representatives of the Kingdom of God— ambassadors for Christ. If we behave like such and announce what our King sent us to do, and we perform His works, people will listen to us.

Another revealing and important point is that when an ambassador of a foreign nation is sent, the one sending him is responsible

216 | The Kingdom of God and Its Righteousness

to supply whatever he needs to make his mission successful. We are sent by the King of kings and our provision comes from the Kingdom—to which we belong.

- **We are like Jesus**

"¹⁷Love has been perfected among us in this: that we may have boldness in the day of judgment; because as He is, so are we in this world." 1 John 4.17

- **We will do the same works as He did**

"¹²Most assuredly, I say to you, he who believes in Me, the works that I do he will do also; and greater works than these he will do, because I go to My Father..." John 14.12

We are ambassadors for Jesus, sent with His power to perform even greater works than He did.

Whom will we share the message with?

The message of the Kingdom and the cross is for the poor, the captives, the oppressed, the sick, the blind, junkies, the career-minded, the respectable, the homeless, and skilled workers; for the Black, White, Hispanic, rich, tall, and short; for men, women, children, young adults, and the elderly—everyone!

What are we going to do?

Like Jesus, our job is to preach, teach, heal, and rebuke demons; to practice both parts of the gospel of the Kingdom, the Word, and His works.

"¹⁷And these signs will follow those who believe: In My name they will cast out demons; they will speak with new tongues; ¹⁸they will take up

serpents; and if they drink anything deadly, it will by no means hurt them; they will lay hands on the sick, and they will recover."
Mark 16.17, 18

Who will go with us?

The Holy Spirit of God will give us the power, boldness, authority, and will confirm, with miracles, whatever we may declare.

"²⁰And they went out and preached everywhere, the Lord working with them and confirming the word through the accompanying signs. Amen."
Mark 16.20

What are we to pray for?

The ambassador of the Kingdom of God should always be well prepared. One way to do this is to establish a well-rooted prayer life which includes specifics regarding the mission he was sent to do, including:

* For God to open doors.

  "³...meanwhile praying also for us, that God would open to us a door for the word, to speak the mystery of Christ, for which I am also in chains..." Colossians 4.3

* For the Holy Spirit to give us divine appointments.

* For God to prepare us every day so we can have the ability to speak to others about the gospel.

* For the veil to be removed from people's eyes. The gospel of the Kingdom can only be understood by revelation brought upon by the Holy Spirit.

  "¹¹But I make known to you, brethren, that the gospel which was preached by me is not according to man. ¹²For I neither received it

from man, nor was I taught it, but it came through the revelation of Jesus Christ." Galatians 1.11, 12

- For people's understanding to be opened, because people with a free mind, cannot reject the gospel of the Kingdom of God.

"³But even if our gospel is veiled, it is veiled to those who are perishing, ⁴whose minds the god of this age has blinded, who do not believe, lest the light of the gospel of the glory of Christ, who is the image of God, should shine on them." 2 Corinthians 4.3, 4

What weapons are at our disposal?

Jesus gave us many weapons and resources to carry out our commission. Therefore, we must not fear when we preach the gospel of the Kingdom. This arsenal includes: the anointing of the Holy Spirit, the spiritual armor of the Lord, the name of Jesus, the Word, prayer, faith, authority, power, His blood, and the gifts of the Holy Spirit.

When is it time to go and share the gospel?

Now is the time!

"²Preach the word! Be ready in season and out of season. Convince, rebuke, exhort, with all longsuffering and teaching. ⁵But you be watchful in all things, endure afflictions, do the work of an evangelist, fulfill your ministry." 2 Timothy 4.2, 5

Who will go in His name?

"¹⁴How then shall they call on Him in whom they have not believed? And how shall they believe in Him of whom they have not heard? And how shall they hear without a preacher? ¹⁵And how shall they preach unless they are sent? As it is written: "How beautiful are the feet of those who preach the gospel of peace, who bring glad tidings of good things!" Romans 10.14, 15

We should answer the call by saying, "Here I am Lord, and I will go. I will put on the footwear of the gospel of peace and announce your

Word." The harvest is ready. The multitudes thirst for the good news of the Kingdom. The souls are ready to receive the Lord and His Kingdom. God is counting on you!

The great army of God is composed of men
and women who are passionate for His cause
and armed with authority, power,
and the gifts of the Holy Spirit.

Chapter 10

THE HOLY SPIRIT, THE BELIEVER, AND THE EXPANSION OF THE KINGDOM

God's goal is to establish His Kingdom on Earth. This was also Jesus' greatest passion during the three and a half years of His ministry. Today, we see this divine legacy continue with the Holy Spirit, who seeks men and women with a heart for warfare and who can share God's passion for the Kingdom of God to be set forth.

It is time for war, not peace. The time has come to gather the harvest; but beware, there is an enemy who will do whatever it takes to stop this. Consequently, the Holy Spirit is leading His people into battle— to fight for the establishment of God's Kingdom, on Earth.

It is pertinent that we learn from this Israelite nation...

When they left Egypt, they were only a few days from the Promised Land. At the verge of seeing their promise fulfilled, their Philistine enemies rose up to stand in their way; this meant they would have to fight for their promise.

"¹⁷Then it came to pass, when Pharaoh had let the people go, that God did not lead them by way of the land of the Philistines, although that was near; for God said, "Lest perhaps the people change their minds when they see war, and return to Egypt." Exodus 13.17

After surveying the land God had promised them, they felt it was impossible to fight and win, for the people who occupied it were re-portedly "giants" and as a Philistine city it was known to be "strongly fortified." Unfortunately, they allowed this report to determine their inability to fight.

Prior, God had allowed them to journey through the desert for two years—ample time to experience the struggles of the desert—yet, they still chose to believe that conquering the Philistines land would be too great a struggle to surrender before actually facing battle—they chose to die in the desert. Unfortunately, since that generation refused to step forward and fight for their inheritance, they were unable to enjoy God's Promised Land. Things are still the same today. Many believers prefer to die in the desert instead of choosing to fight for their God-given promises.

That generation of Israelites turned their backs to God's promises and died in the desert because they were *not ready for war*.

―――――――――― ༻✦༺ ――――――――――
The Holy Spirit is leading His people into battle;
to fight for the establishment of God's Kingdom, on Earth.
―――――――――― ༻✦༺ ――――――――――

Illustration: Between 1963 and 1968, the enemy implemented his attack against the United States; his plan was to stop the knowledge of God from spreading. A few of his strategies were: the assassination of John F. Kennedy, stopping prayer in schools, and spreading sexual immorality through propaganda aimed at the youth. A clear example of the latter is the *hippie* movement which caused wide-spread rebellion among the youth, destroyed moral values, and the institution of marriage and family. As these events took place, there was not a single Christian in sight to stand up and counterattack the enemy. Undeniably, that generation lacked the Spirit and heart for war.

In the Old Testament, we saw how the entire generation of cowards with slave mentalities who chose not to fight lost their lives; only a small remnant survived: Joshua and Caleb. God gave these two men the opportunity to lead a kingdom of priests into war because He saw they had a different spirit: they were warriors *ready to conquer* the land.

"³Every place that the sole of your foot will tread upon I have given you, as I said to Moses." Joshua 1.3

The phrase "tread upon" comes from the Hebrew word *darak* which means: to string a bow by treading on it in bending; to tread, bend, bent, lead, archer, step down, come, and go; to stride upon, walk, drew, lead forth, guide, tread out, go over, shoot, or thresh. Often, this word is translated to imply the following: to bend a bow using the foot to prepare it and have it ready for action. At times, it means to *lock and load* the weapons in preparation for combat.

With this explanation in mind, we could re-read the previous verse the following way: "That which you prepare your arsenal against, and go forth, like an aggressive army that aims to possess, is what I have given them." In other words, "You will not gain an inch of that land if you are not willing to fight for it. I gave it to you, but you will not take possession if you choose not to fight."

If we study the generation of the Sixties, we notice they were not a generation of warriors willing to fight against institutions or demonic spirits. However, at the beginning of this millennium, that generation ends and a new one begins. Now is the time when a youth filled with the spirit for warfare will step up and conquer the Promised Land.

The Kingdom of God must be imparted, not forced, so the new generation of warriors can continue carrying forth its legacy.

In the history of the church, we find John, the beloved disciple, training and imparting the Kingdom to a generation of young warriors. With them, he successfully accomplished the great assault on the city of Ephesus.

"¹³I write to you, fathers, because you have known Him who is from the beginning. I write to you, young men, because you have overcome the wicked one. I write to you, little children, because you have known the Father."
1 John 2.13

One of these great warriors was, Polycarp. John visited the Greek temple of the goddess Artemisia where the Roman goddess Diana was also worshipped—both are the same spirit. Polycarp's writings teach that when John stood in the temple and declared justice against the goddess Diana, the altar instantly disintegrated into hundreds of pieces and a third of the temple—what used to be one of the seven wonders of the ancient world—was destroyed.

Up until that point, everyone would proclaim, "The goddess Diana is great!" After the temple was destroyed, the heavens were opened over the city of Ephesus, the people converted to Jesus, and they changed their confession to, "John worships a great God!" Overnight, the city of Ephesus converted. For over fifty years, they had worshipped the Roman goddess, Diana, but after the temple was destroyed, the entire city worshipped Jesus, the Son of God.

Today, our cities are full of immorality, injustice, and idolatry. Moral values in our society have deteriorated and things are only getting worse. This is why we are compelled to extend the Kingdom and establish it in our hearts, families, churches, city, and across the nations. But before we can accomplish this great task, we must learn to achieve the phases required in establishing and extending the Kingdom of God on Earth.

Four phases on the advancement of the Kingdom, on Earth

Like every other government, the Kingdom of God has strategies or phases of advancement, establishing, development, and expansion. Let us study these strategic methods of advancement for the eternal Kingdom.

1. **Preaching or proclaiming the Kingdom *without* the visible demonstration of power.**

    This is the first phase that takes place in the Kingdom of God, and it has to do with teaching, announcing, and proclaiming the Kingdom with words but without demonstrations of power—as John the Baptist did. He never performed a miracle or a supernatural sign or wonder. He announced the coming of the Kingdom but never established nor demonstrated it, because that would take place with Jesus.

"41Then many came to Him and said, "John performed no sign, but all the things that John spoke about this Man were true." John 10.41

Most churches and ministries stop at the point where John was: performing neither signs nor wonders. However, today, this should not be the case because with Jesus' coming we were empowered; we no longer have excuses for remaining stagnant and unable to perform signs. Although these churches and ministries do a good job at teaching and preaching the Kingdom, they rebuke evil but fail to manifest tangible evidence of the Kingdom's power, which includes, among its many virtues, the power to heal the sick.

Let us remember that the gospel of the Kingdom includes proclaiming the good news *and* taking a corresponding action—words and power go hand in hand. If these two ingredients are missing, it is not the gospel of the Kingdom. John the Baptist preached the gospel without being equipped by the Holy Spirit to rebuke demons and demonstrate the power of the new government. Consequently, he was imprisoned and decapitated for preaching the Kingdom of God. He was the first to die in the war because the territory he entered was occupied.

John the Baptist came in the power of Elijah's spirit, but that anointing was not sufficient to overcome and destroy the principalities and strongholds of his time. In the end, he was defeated by the spirit of Jezebel. Elijah suffered the same fate. However, Elisha came with the double anointing: the apostolic and prophetic, which was powerful enough to destroy Jezebel and accomplish what Elijah was unable to do. Thousands of years later, Jesus came as the great Elisha. He crossed the line of preaching with mere words and entered the second stage which includes demonstration.

2. Preaching the Kingdom *with* the visible demonstration of power

When John the Baptist finished preaching the Kingdom of God, the new order of Jesus was established. He preached, taught, and demonstrated the Kingdom of God with miracles, healing, signs, wonders, and by casting out demons; the latter had never been seen prior to Jesus' coming. The Son of God was the first Man with the authority to rebuke demons from people's minds and bodies. With Jesus, the Kingdom was widespread and established throughout the land with visible demonstrations of God's power.

How did Jesus cross the line that separates words from visible actions?

Jesus stated, "Only the violent take the Kingdom by force," because, He, crossed the line by force. My dear friend, in case you did not know, this is a war between kingdoms: the government of God against the government of darkness. Therefore, we can no longer pretend to carry out our mission peacefully. The adversary has trespassed into our territory and intends to stay at all costs. Therefore, we have no choice but to force him out and establish a new government; but this can only occur as we seek and rely on the help and power of the Spirit of War, better known as the Holy Spirit—He is the essence of God.

In our time, many believers are *stuck* in the first stage; they are unable to extend the Kingdom in their territory because they fear the enemy. Instead of evicting him, they make peace with him and settle for a "permit" that allows them to establish a religion in his territory. They still call themselves *Christians* but do not execute their title with power. They speak of a far away Kingdom—a future Kingdom—without impacting the present one.

The Kingdom of God is here and now, through us.
We cannot negotiate with the enemy. He has to vacate!

Jesus preached the Kingdom with a visible demonstration of God's power. He was obedient and lived under the delegated authority of His Father who allowed Him to express the Kingdom in word and action. However, even that authority was limited by this earthly realm because Jesus had not resurrected yet. The

Messiah's resurrection contained a secret that would loosen His power against the strongholds of the kingdom of darkness, resulting in a change in the airs.

"²⁴But that you may know that the Son of Man has power on Earth to forgive sins"—He said to the man who was paralyzed, "I say to you, arise, take up your bed, and go to your house." Luke 5.24

In this stage of preaching and proclaiming the Kingdom, Jesus operated under the authority that derives as a direct result of obedience. This type of authority is limited to Earth and can only be gained by submitting to authority. In other words, if we are obedient, we will also rise to that same level. Jesus demonstrated the Kingdom as a man while under absolute obedience to His Father. The battle He won in the desert was crucial victory, marking the beginning of the manifested Kingdom of God on Earth. In other words, the phase of proclaiming the Kingdom with tangible demonstrations of God's dominion was kindled during that victory.

Jesus was far from satisfied. At the time, He was the only instrument of God that carried out this task; the only one who preached and demonstrated the Kingdom. The double-edged sword flowed from His lips and was effective in His hands, every word and action He took was a demonstration of His power and a representation of the Kingdom, both by word and action! All it took was the sound of His voice or movement of the hands for powerful miracles to take place; nevertheless, He knew that *more* would be required to finish God's work.

As a result, during His three and a half years in ministry, He experienced a great level of frustration. He was the sole provider; He did everything. There was so much to do. In between Him spending long periods of time in prayer and meeting the people's needs, there was barely any time to eat or rest. The multitude was immense, He could not do the work alone, and so He sent out His twelve disciples.

"¹Then He called His twelve disciples together and gave them power and authority over all demons, and to cure diseases." Luke 9.1

The twelve men extended the Kingdom in the same manner as Jesus: They proclaimed it with the visible demonstration of God's power, including healing the sick and casting out demons. But, the need was so great and the work so extensive that Jesus decided to commission another seventy.

"¹After these things the Lord appointed seventy others also, and sent them two by two before His face into every city and place where He Himself was about to go." Luke 10.1

The seventy carried out their mission, they returned rejoicing because the sick were healed, the demon-oppressed were delivered, and the Kingdom of God advanced with greater force.

"¹⁷Then the seventy returned with joy, saying, "Lord, even the demons are subject to us in Your name." ²⁰Nevertheless do not rejoice in this, that the spirits are subject to you, but rather rejoice because your names are written in heaven." Luke 10.17, 20

After hearing the enemy was rebuked and cast out of the territory, Jesus rejoiced!

"²¹In that hour, Jesus rejoiced in the Spirit..." Luke 10.21

Luke is the only place in Scripture that tells of Jesus rejoicing. Something extraordinarily powerful occurred in His Spirit as He heard the disciple's report, causing Him to rejoice.

From that day, Jesus continued to extend the Kingdom with 82 men, but even these were not enough to supply all of the people's needs. Regardless of the advances made, He continued to feel frustrated because of His inability to advance the Kingdom with power and authority to its fullest extent. Jesus felt restricted.

"⁴⁹I came to send fire on the Earth, and how I wish it were already kindled! ⁵⁰But I have a baptism to be baptized with and how distressed I am till it is accomplished!" Luke 12.49, 50

In the previous verse, we find two important words: *distressed* and *baptism*. In Greek, the word for distressed is *synochē*; it means: a holding together, a narrowing, or the contracting part of a way. Metaphorically speaking, it means: straits, distress, or anguish.

In those days, Jesus experienced a sense of restriction, frustration, and anguish because the Kingdom was unable to flow as it should. He felt this way because He was yet to accomplish His calling: to be crucified and resurrected. Although He was extending the Kingdom, He was only in the *second phase* of advancement: preaching the Word with demonstrations of power.

The baptism Jesus spoke of in *Luke 12.50*, is different to the ones in water or the Spirit: It is a baptism of "suffering:" the blood-shedding experience He would soon endure through the betrayal, abuse, and crucifixion process. He probably thought to Himself: "When I die at the cross and am raised from the dead, I will ignite the Earth on fire!"

Jesus' resurrection included the power
that would loosen His authority
to operate in the Heavens.

During the "second phase," Jesus was able to manifest the Kingdom as the first man who lived under absolute obedience to the Father and by the Father's delegated authority. He recovered the authority Adam had lost; thus, able to forgive sin, heal the sick, cast out demons, and control nature. However, His sphere of authority was still limited to Earth, not Heaven. Due to this limitation, He was unable to destroy the principalities and strongholds of the air—yet. This would only be made possible after His death and resurrection.

Today, most people in the body of Christ move in the first level of advancement: preaching *without* the demonstration of God's power. Another percentage operates in the second stage of advancement: preaching or proclaiming the Word *with* a visible demonstration of God's power. In general, the worldwide church is moving at this level, but it still lacks clear, strong, and defined manifestation of the Kingdom or government of God on Earth. We know this to be true because most cities around the world suffer due to the lack of justice, peace, and joy. In addition, we find drug addiction, idolatry, witchcraft, crime, abortion, immorality, lasciviousness, and more. There is not one city where we can find peace, justice, and the fullness of God's glory. During this second phase of advancement, we are unable to win entire cities for Jesus. Nonetheless, the Lord does promise, in His Word, that we will restore the cities and future generations. Jesus was unable to do a complete restoration during His ministry on Earth, because it was still only the second phase of Kingdom advancement.

"⁴And they shall build the old wastes, they shall raise up the former desolations, and they shall repair the waste cities, the desolations of many generations." Isaiah 61.4

So then, how will *we* do it? Before we can answer this key question, let us take a closer look at Jesus during the three and a half years He spent in Jerusalem. There, He preached, taught, healed the sick, and cast out demons. The miracles He performed were the most powerful and extraordinary miracles ever seen by human eyes. One of the most impressive miracles Jesus performed was raising his dear friend from the dead. It was four days after Lazarus' death, his body was well into the process of decomposition, yet that did not stop Jesus. He boldly called Lazarus to come out of the tomb. Immediately Lazarus was brought back to life! One would never imagine that at the sight of such grand demonstration of limitless power, witnesses would react with scorn and hate for Jesus—nonetheless, they did. They wanted to kill Jesus (and Lazarus). The priests and leaders of Israel agreed to put Him to death, as a means of stopping Him from performing further miracles, signs, and wonders, and as a way to discourage the people from following Him.

During His ministry, the multitudes followed Him. If they were sick, He healed them. If they were hungry, He fed them. The blind could see, the deaf could hear, the lame could walk, the lepers were cleansed, and the dead were brought back to life. However, after three and a half years, the city showed no signs of significant change. Accordingly, at the end of Jesus' ministry on Earth, only 120 people were truly committed to His cause.

The lack of change in Jerusalem had nothing to do with Jesus' ministry. The principles and strongholds that dominated the city were responsible for hindering the advancement of the Kingdom of God. These strongholds governed the city and needed to be eliminated. This victory could only occur, however, when Jesus would go to the cross and then resurrect—equating to Satan's total defeat. Jesus also had to ascend to Heaven, sit on the throne—at the right hand of the Father—and begin to exercise dominion and authority through the Holy Spirit.

Interestingly enough, the same takes place today. The cities are in darkness; full of sin, crime, and idolatry. Churches proclaim the gospel, heal the sick, and cast out demons, but the cities never experience positive change because the church has failed to destroy the strongholds and principalities that govern the air. Consequently, the Kingdom cannot be established in a clear, powerful, or defined way.

> We gain nothing by having a church that is on fire,
> if the city is controlled by Satan.

Illustration: Many ministries experience the joy of people coming to the altar by the hundreds, but the following month, only half of those new believers continue to attend. In other churches, five people are healed of cancer but three die the next month. Others water baptize a hundred but half return to the world. The church grows for one or two weeks but soon after stops growing, with the same cycle taking place year after year. The leadership grows and matures until a leader attacks the pastor, speaks ill of him, and decides to leave the church and take half the congregation with him. This is an endless war because the principalities and strongholds of that city or region are resisting the advancement of the Kingdom—precisely why they *must* be vanquished!

Jesus was dissatisfied and grieved while at the second phase of advancement. He looked forward to the future to a time when, after His resurrection, the Earth could be set ablaze by the fire of the Holy Spirit. Unfortunately, He had to wait until His *baptism of suffering*.

3. **Advancing the Kingdom with the *power of the resurrection*.**

What type of death did Jesus suffer?

The moment Jesus drank from *His cup* of death, every sinful act found in Adam's bloodline, from the beginning of time to the end, was placed upon Him on the cross.

"24...who Himself bore our sins in His own body on the tree, that we, having died to sins, might live for righteousness—by whose stripes you were healed." 1 Peter 2.24

At the cross, the sinful nature that is imbedded in all of humanity was now imbedded into Jesus. He literally became sin, in the flesh.

"21For He made Him who knew no sin to be sin for us, that we might become the righteousness of God in Him." 2 Corinthians 5.21

Every sin committed by Adam and his descendants was deposited on Jesus' body, turning His soul into the recipient of Adam's sinful nature.

"56The sting of death is sin, and the strength of sin is the law." 1 Corinthians 15.56

His crucifixion fulfilled the curse and the sting of death (sin). Establishing it as the single event that prevailed all other human events. In this, Jesus became the last Adam.

"⁴⁵And so it is written, "The first man Adam became a living being." The last Adam became a life-giving spirit." 1 Corinthians 15.45

His stay on Earth turned into sin's focal point, the garbage disposal for every sin committed by Adam and his descendants. This is what *His cup* contained.

God's wrath against Adam and his descendants' sin (from the beginning to the end of time) was laid unto Jesus. The One who afflicted, punished, and hurt Jesus, was God. The relationship between Father and Son was completely destroyed at the cross, while the cost of sin was paid. The Jews and Roman soldiers were merely the instruments of His wrath.

"¹⁰Yet, it pleased the LORD to bruise Him; He has put Him to grief. When You make His soul an offering for sin, He shall see His seed, He shall prolong His days, and the pleasure of the LORD shall prosper in His hand." Isaiah 53.10

When His suffering was complete, Jesus cried out: "It is finished." This phrase comes from the Greek word *teleo*, which means: to end, complete, execute, conclude; to release a debt, pay, satisfy, finish, consummate, fulfill. In other words, there was nothing left that needed to be paid. His outcry was a shout of victory not pain. The wages of sin had been completely satisfied. It was then that Jesus surrendered His Spirit and died. When the centurion standing next to the cross realized that Jesus was in complete charge and control of His own execution, even up to the moment of His death, he knelt down completely astonished and said, "Truly, this is the Son of God."

When and **how** did Jesus receive the miracle of His resurrection? Jesus received His resurrection by faith, at the Garden of Gethsemane, *before* surrendering to the cross.

"7...who, in the days of His flesh, when He had offered up prayers and supplications, with vehement cries and tears to Him who was able to save Him from death, and was heard because of His godly fear..."
Hebrews 5.7

Nearing His death, Jesus prayed to be delivered and was heard. Hallelujah!

The Son of God died with an exponential level of sin casted unto Him—the aggregate sin of mankind was laid upon His shoulders. Sin had clinged onto Him, a stronghold was created, giving death the power to hold Him back more than any other man. Respectively, if there was one man who never could have been raised from the dead, it was Jesus. Nevertheless, He was raised by the glory of His Father.

Unlike, Lazarus, who remained the same man after being resurrected, Jesus, was *very different* after His resurrection. As the last Adam, He died with the sin of humanity upon His shoulders and overpowered death once and for all. Once raised from the dead, Jesus was made new, He arose as: Lord of Heaven, the One whom neither Satan nor hell can hold back.

"3For I delivered to you first of all that which I also received: that Christ died for our sins according to the Scriptures, 4and that He was buried, and that He rose again the third day according to the Scriptures..."
1 Corinthians 15.3, 4

Satan never could and never will be able to touch this new Being. When Jesus was raised from the dead, none of the sins with which He died remained. He left behind every transgression at the tomb. Sin could no longer affect His new glorious life—this is the power and glory of the resurrection.

Through the law of inheritance, everyone is able to partake of every stage in Jesus' life: His suffering, crucifixion, death, and resurrection. We were upon His loins, like Levi was upon Abraham's loins (Hebrews 7.10). In other words, we are recipients of every benefit and blessing that comes from His passion, suffering, and resurrection.

The true power of the resurrection
is not simply the physical miracle of raising Jesus
from the dead, but the cleansing of the sin that condemned us.

Jesus was raised from the dead and placed on the throne of glory. As He was renewed, He received legal power and authority over Satan and his power, with the right to cast him out and destroy his kingdom and works against God's creation. Jesus was also raised to sit in heavenly places with the authority to reign powerfully in Heaven and on Earth. This was true then and will continue to be true for eternity.

"18And Jesus came and spoke to them, saying, "All authority has been given to Me in heaven and on Earth." Matthew 28.18

Jesus' new position, power, and authority empowered the disciples to go throughout the land preaching the resurrection of Jesus. Although this was an amazing miracle, what really changed the disciples' lives and the world, was the power that was loosened by His resurrection—the same power that changes us today.

To whom did Jesus delegate the authority and power that He conquered at His resurrection?

While Jesus ascended to His throne in Heaven, He delegated the governing power and authority He received at His resurrection to the church.

"22And He put all things under His feet, and gave Him to be head over all things to the church." Ephesians 1.22

Correspondently, the disciples received the baptism of the Holy Spirit in the Upper Room. Here, they received the authority and power of Christ's resurrection. This was the catalyst that caused them to immediately gather the harvest and destroy the city's principalities and strongholds; the Kingdom of God was proclaimed and manifested throughout Jerusalem.

The first harvest was when Peter preached during the Pentecostal Celebration and three thousand people were saved and added to the Kingdom and the church. Later, When Peter preached again, a lame man walked and an additional five thousand people were added to the church; two years later, a third of the population in Jerusalem was saved. In other words, over twenty thousand were saved in a very short time.

Peter's harvest was a direct result of Jesus' resurrection power being delegated onto him. Jesus, did not destroy the principalities and strongholds in Jerusalem, rather this was a task given and accomplished by His disciples. Consequently, no one can say, "Jesus preached the gospel with supernatural *power* because He was the Son of God." The disciples, common men like you and I, were responsible for the harvest of souls gathered in Jerusalem. They exemplify what it means to "take over the city"—no more excuses! WE CAN TOO.

Our churches need revelation from the Holy Spirit, so they may proclaim the gospel with the demonstration of power that came with Jesus' resurrection. With *it*, they will gather the harvest—rejoicing at the sight of cities and nations being transformed and restored to the Kingdom's original design.

*"10...that I may know Him and **the power of His resurrection**, and the fellowship of His sufferings, being conformed to His death..."*
Philippians 3.10

Paul's great desire was to know Jesus intimately, have revelation of the *power of His resurrection,* and *to* conquer the world, for Jesus, with the gospel of the Kingdom. The disciples spent their lives preaching *and* performing signs and wonders—which are inherent results of preaching with the *power of the resurrection.*

The law of inheritance transfers Adam's sin and condemns us for its transgression

Adam's disobedience manifests in our lives as an inherited sin (or the original sin). The law of inheritance teaches that we were in Adam when he sinned. Therefore, through Adam, all men inherited the consequences of sin. His disobedience manifests as inherited sin, family curses, and witchcraft and the occult. Curses result from practicing masonry and primitive ceremonies; they can be national and regional curses practiced or imposed by our ancestors and cultural traditions, including: ancestral worship and honoring the dead—both are demonic curses. Only the power of the cross can deliver us from these curses precisely because it was at the cross that Jesus became a curse for us.

"[13]Christ has redeemed us from the curse of the law, having become a curse for us (for it is written, 'Cursed is everyone who hangs on a tree')" *Galatians 3.13*

After Jesus' sacrifice, the law of inheritance worked wonderfully in our favor because we can individually receive the benefits of the cross through our faith in Christ. The malign inheritance we received from Adam was taken from us at the cross, replacing it with the inheritance from the risen Christ.

In Christ, we are delivered of every curse imposed by those who hate or hated our ancestors, and we are free of the consequences attached to their involvement in the occult and their choice to live independently of God.

Let us read the following passage slowly and carefully:

"[1]What shall we say then? Shall we continue in sin that grace may abound? [2]Certainly not! How shall we who died to sin live any longer in

it? ³Or do you not know that as many of us as were baptized into Christ Jesus were baptized into His death? ⁴Therefore we were buried with Him through baptism into death, that just as Christ was raised from the dead by the glory of the Father, even so we also should walk in newness of life. ⁵For if we have been united together in the likeness of His death, certainly we also shall be in the likeness of His resurrection..." Romans 6.1-5

Throughout the Bible, especially in the books of Romans, Ephesians, and Colossians, we see the words, "in Him" or "together with Him" are read over and over again. Yes, we were in Christ when He became sin and paid its wages. We were also in Him when He was buried and raised from the dead.

4. Advancing the Kingdom by force

This is the most violent phase of the war. The conflict between the Kingdom of God and the kingdom of darkness is a violent collision of powers. In this phase, we preach, teach, demonstrate, **and** extend the Kingdom throughout our territories.

Illustration: Once, a radical Muslim asked a Christian: "Are you one of those Christians who speak in tongues, heal the sick, and perform miracles?" The Christian responded affirmatively; then the Muslim said, "Your kind is the only one we fear."

When we speak about extending the Kingdom by force, we should understand exactly what we are doing and with whom we are dealing with. The advancement of the Kingdom is an ongoing aggression; it is a war that cannot be won without a certain degree of aggressiveness.

God calls us when it is time to attack. When we begin to extend the Kingdom by force, the devil perceives it as a declaration of war and begins his attack; this is our cue to increase and sustain our offensive and violent assault by casting out demons, healing the sick, delivering the captives, and healing the brokenhearted. The Holy Spirit, or the Spirit of war, extends the Kingdom through us; this is the same Spirit that led Jesus to the desert to be tempted, to fight Satan, and to defeat him with the power of the Word.

To enter the Kingdom, enjoy it, and make it come to us, is directly related to the power of the Holy Spirit. The key of the Kingdom to govern the Earth is invisible but operates in the visible realm. As long as the Holy Spirit dwells in us, the Kingdom of God will continually be established on Earth; this makes it possible for God to govern. In other words, God governs through the Holy Spirit—an invisible being operating in an invisible human spirit that lives in a visible human body, on Earth. This means that the Holy Spirit in us brings the Kingdom to Earth. Therefore, if He dwells in us, the Kingdom, and everything it contains—justice, peace, joy, power, order, fatherhood, love, obedience, and more—added to the will of God, has to manifest through us, daily.

This is the same Spirit that anointed Jesus at the moment of His baptism to declare the good news of the gospel. In the gospel of John, Jesus teaches that His works are performed by the Father in Him, but the gospel of Luke says these works are performed by the Holy Spirit that dwells in Him. What we understand with this is that the Father, as well as the Holy Spirit, worked in cooperation with Him because the three are One. The same happens with us, the believers.

"[38]...how God anointed Jesus of Nazareth with the Holy Spirit and with power, who went about doing good and healing all who were oppressed by the devil, for God was with Him." Acts 10.38

The agent of God in charge of manifesting the Kingdom of God on Earth is the Holy Spirit, but He too, needs a human body to implement the principles of the Kingdom. Only humanity has the legal right to operate on Earth and give legality to the leadings and actions of the Holy Spirit. God established this principle in His Word. Therefore, He is the first to respect and obey this principle, fully.

After Jesus was baptized and the Holy Spirit came upon Him, He began to establish the Kingdom by casting out demons; in other words, removing the kingdom of darkness in order to establish the Kingdom of God.

"20But if I cast out demons with the finger of God, surely the Kingdom of God has come upon you." Luke 11.20

The finger of God is a sign of authority and absolute power; when it is pointed, it defeats His enemies and brings victory to the children of the Kingdom.

As soon as Jesus began casting demons out, the Pharisees (religious men who rejected the power of the Holy Spirit and the supernatural) criticized Him. What did Jesus refer to when He mentioned *the finger of God*? This expression is another way to say: "By the Holy Spirit." In the Old Testament, it is only mentioned once, in Exodus.

"19Then the magicians said to Pharaoh, "This is the finger of God." Exodus 8.19

To fully understand the expression *the finger of God*, let us briefly review the context of this verse. Exodus 8 covers the time when Moses and Aaron told the Egyptian Pharaoh to let the Israelite nation go free, but while God sent Moses with signs and wonders of power, He also hardened the Pharaoh's heart; the effect of this was the Pharaoh's determination to keep the people in bondage. Up to that point, Pharaoh's magicians were able to duplicate everything God did through Moses and Aaron's spoken word. However, when a *creative* miracle takes place, the supremacy of God becomes evident. When the Lord turned dust into lice, the magicians and sorcerers implemented their efforts and knowledge to try and equal the miracle but were unsuccessful. When they gave up trying, they realized there was nothing else they could do except to recognize, before the Pharaoh and Moses, that the miracle could not have been performed by any other than the *finger of God*. In essence, even the magicians and sorcerers recognized the existence of a God that was far more powerful than the one they served. However, the Pharaoh, blinded by pride and stubbornness, rejected that notion.

Up to that point, Moses had performed miracles by the *words of faith* spoken to him by God. After this last sign, Moses takes a step back because the Lord had personally entered the battle. This caused the magicians to fear and recognize that they were no longer fighting two men, but God—a great and powerful God!

What is the *finger of God*?

The *finger of God* is the Holy Spirit clothed in a human body, fighting the battle God sends us to fight. When the Kingdom is proclaimed, the Holy Spirit enters the battle by taking our humanity and turning us into the *finger of God*.

Jesus' last declaration before ascending into Heaven was in reference to receiving the Holy Spirit. He said the Holy Spirit would empower us to exercise the Father's will on Earth and turn us into the *finger of God*—soldiers capable of destroying His enemies.

"⁴⁹Behold, I send the Promise of My Father upon you; but tarry in the city of Jerusalem until you are endued with power from on high." Luke 24.49

People need the Kingdom because it represents power. Today, everyone, including you and I, seek power. People work hard trying to improve their lifestyles and standard of living through school and careers; they lose sleep trying to overcome their inferior conditions and take control of the circumstances affecting their lives. People are convinced they can find power in intellectualism, business, science, wealth, fame, or others; however, true power can only be given by the Holy Spirit, and received by us when we enter the Kingdom. The key to extending the government of God is to allow the Holy Spirit to dwell in us and turn us into the *finger of God*. With the Holy Spirit in us, we can cast out demons and dethrone Satan from every territory. Let us follow our King's command to conquer!

How does the Holy Spirit extend the Kingdom of God?

The only way to extend the Kingdom is by *force*. Every time the gospel of the Kingdom is taught and preached, a declaration of war is made against the kingdom of darkness. Consequently, we must be ready to fight the enemy because he *will* resist. In the gospel of Matthew, Jesus made a declaration using key words: *endured, violent, seize, and force.* This is an indication that the establishment of the Kingdom of God, on Earth, involves a violent action.

*"¹²And from the days of John the Baptist until the present time, the Kingdom of heaven has **endured** violent assault, and **violent** men **seize** it by **force** [as a precious prize—a share in the heavenly Kingdom is sought with most ardent zeal and intense exertion]." Matthew 11.12—AMP*

Depending on the translation, this verse can be interpreted in different ways. For a better understanding of its meaning, it is preferable to consult the Greek manuscript. There, the verb *suffer* is in passive voice; this means that a more exact translation would be: *"A violent act has incurred against the Kingdom, but the Kingdom has reacted violently, advancing by force."*

Another way to say this is: Wherever the Kingdom manifests, it is then violently assaulted by Satan, particularly, in the beginning stage. This is true because what Satan fears the most are the demonstrations of power performed in Jesus' Kingdom. He does not fear anything else. Any manifestation of the Kingdom of God is a mortal threat to Satan. Jesus taught us that before John the Baptist, no one on Earth had preached the Kingdom. The moment Jesus began establishing God's government, every demonic power was sent against Him; this is why Jesus counterattacked with even greater force: In the desert, He rebuked Satan with the Word and when He preached, He cast demons out of people and established the Kingdom in them. This is violent!

It is important to understand this is the only way to advance the Kingdom of God. We cannot do it peacefully; we must be violent men and women of God. Jesus was the first courageous Man who attacked the kingdom of darkness, offensively. The further we advance the Kingdom of God, counterattacking the powers of darkness, preaching, healing, and casting out demons, the more authority we gain; this is referred to as gained authority.

Illustration: In the beginning, when I was first practicing deliverance—casting out demons—and healing the sick, it would take a long time. Now, due to extensive battlefield experience, I have gained a greater level of authority and power. This makes it possible for me to cast out demons in a matter of seconds and for people to receive their healing, almost always, instantaneously. I no longer have to practice one-on-one ministry. I simply declare the Word and massive deliverances and healing occur. Consequently, I am able to extend the Kingdom at a greater speed than before.

The kingdom of Satan can only operate
where the Kingdom of God has not arrived
because both cannot coexist.

The kingdom of darkness knows it must retreat when the Kingdom of God arrives. Furthermore, wherever the divine government of God is established, Satan cannot afflict those who are under total submission and obedience to the Father (submission and obedience made Jesus impenetrable). When the Kingdom of God is established in the family, church, or city, the kingdom of darkness stops and the devil is no longer able to inflict his evil deeds. This takes place because the children of the Kingdom have taken from the devil the legal right to operate in that territory.

Any advance made by the government of God is an invasion against Satan's territory. On this planet there are no vacant "lots," everything, everyplace, and everyone, are occupied by either Satan's kingdom or God's Kingdom. Since every "parcel of land" is occupied, when the Kingdom of God advances, Satan defends his territory at all costs. As a general rule, there will instinctively be a demonic reaction whenever the Kingdom manifests. This is the underlying cause for the violence endured by God's Kingdom.

Through which *doors* will the Kingdom extend?

"18And I also say to you that you are Peter, and on this rock I will build My church, and the gates of Hades shall not prevail against it." Matthew 16.18

What *doors* are we referring to? Architects would build cities with protective walls that measured 30 feet wide and 100 feet high; this wall would include a massive door every couple of feet.

These massive doors served two principal functions:

- To provide an entry and exit point for business people, soldiers, and citizens.

- To exercise justice, judgment, and government over the citizens living within its walls. The elders would sit by each door and controlled who entered and exited the city.

Today, we do not have fortified cities with massive walls and doors, but every capital city is considered the point of entry to countries or towns. Satan understands the power these doors represent, and he has established himself in these cities, making them his centers of power. Throughout the world, almost without exception, every capital city is a stronghold supported and fed by the kingdom of darkness that must be taken back and won for the Kingdom of God!

These cities are also spiritual doors in heavenly places and have the same function: to control and govern the spiritual atmosphere in the surrounding regions, influencing the mentality and behavior of the people. God sent us to conquer and possess the doors of our enemies because through those doors we will establish and extend the Kingdom.

"18In your seed all the nations of the Earth shall be blessed, because you have obeyed My voice." Genesis 22.18

Doors are controlling spheres that generate great influence on the way people think and act. They represent communication, education, politics, the legal and judicial systems, the financial arena, religion, culture, and more.

How can we possess these *doors*?

To possess the *doors*, we must pray for the people in eminence and influential positions; they need to be won for Christ. We must pray for those who sit at the entrance and exit points in our cities. Further, we need to help position people with Christian values so they can be the salt and light of the world and establish God's Kingdom in their cities.

Leaders must make time and use the radio, television, and any other means of communication to preach and extend the Kingdom throughout every city.

What does the Holy Spirit need to extend the Kingdom?

The Holy Spirit is omnipotent. He can do everything God wants Him to do, but remember that the Father decided that a human being should be the one to carry out His wishes on Earth. Therefore, to extend the Kingdom, the Holy Spirit needs the following:

1. A human body

The Holy Spirit is the agent God used to create man. Adam's body was created with the capability to receive His Spirit and breath of life—functions needed to govern the Earth through him and the declaration of his word. Adam's body was created with the ability to receive His Spirit (the breath of life), the instructions on how to govern the Earth, and the ability to hear and declare His Word. God's original intention was for man to govern the Earth; hence, man was given a body. God gave man dominion and lordship to establish His Kingdom here. When God breathed His breath of life upon Adam, it activated him to act in the visible world with the power of an invisible Spirit. God connected man to both worlds.

"¹⁶The heaven, even the heavens, are the LORD's; but the Earth He has given to the children of men." Psalms 115.16

When Adam was connected to the spiritual realm, he received the power to exercise lordship over creation. We should keep in mind that a body without the breath of God cannot govern the Earth. When He comes into our lives, the first area that is activated in us is the spirit of dominion.

"⁷For God has not given us a spirit of fear, but of power and of love and of a sound mind." 2 Timothy 1.7

Illustration: When we are born again and enter the Kingdom of God, the enemy trembles because at that moment we are reconnected with our purpose to execute dominion and lordship; this is our first task: to exercise lordship over all creation. God needs our humanity to advance His Kingdom because He is only able to intervene in man's affairs through another man. If He did it any other way, God would violate His own justice. God needs man to have two essential requisites or virtues:

❖ **Availability**

"⁸Also I heard the voice of the Lord, saying: "Whom shall I send, and who will go for Us?" Then I said, "Here am I! Send me."
Isaiah 6.8

God is not looking for talented, intelligent, wise, rich, or famous men. He is looking for men and women who are available to advance His Kingdom.

God is seeking people who can say,
·Lord, I may not be the best choice
or the most brilliant, but I am available.·

❖ **Obedience**

An obedient person is one who hears with the intention of putting into practice what he hears. God said, "Obedience is better than sacrifice." There are four tests we must overcome to determine if we are obedient: comfort, convenience, beneficial, or reasonable. At the last level, our obedience is proven by fire. If we obey God, even when we do not understand, we prove to be leaders capable of extending His Kingdom. *D.L. Moody* said, "God cannot accomplish anything without people. The world has yet to see what He can do through one man. Lord, allow me to be that *one man*." Many of us follow and love Jesus while the circumstances are comfortable and convenient to do so. However, when circumstances are unreasonable, we are unable to cross the line. Yet, we *can*. We are called to cross that line and serve God even when it does not make sense!

2. A heart for war

When we decide to carry the Kingdom forth, hell comes against our families, businesses, children, and everything else—persecution begins. Our hearts must always be ready for times like this. When we declare war against the enemy in areas such as abortion, sexual immorality, corruption, sin, and when we declare that marriage should be between one man and one woman, and that living a lifestyle without moral values is a sin, be prepared because the kingdom of darkness will come against us.

The generation that walked out of Egypt could have possessed the Promised Land immediately if their hearts had been ready for war. However, instead of dancing, believing God, and taking the land that was rightfully theirs, that generation became afraid, complained, and doubted—these obstacles were self-incurred and became the backbone of their failure to never enter the land and take possession of it.

We are no different than that generation. We want to possess our inheritance without a fight, and when difficult situations demand war, instead of fighting, we complain, murmur, and allow the situation to destroy us. We must fight the war! This is one of many that allow God to show off by demonstrating His power in our favor, and more importantly, allows Him to be: God. He will take care of us during the fight. There is no doubt we will be victorious! The question we must answer is, "Do we have the heart for war?" We will never become soldiers if we settle for being common believers or joyful leaders who prefer comfort to war. Average believers cannot be the answer for their countries and cities if they lack the heart of a warrior; if they do not believe their destiny is to win the war. Remember, we are not referring to a physical war against flesh and blood. Rather, our victory lies in winning the spiritual war against the government of darkness.

"¹Now these are the nations which the LORD left, that He might test Israel by them, that is, all who had not known any of the wars in Canaan ²(this was only so that the generations of the children of Israel might be taught to know war, at least those who had not formerly known it)..." Judges 3.1, 2

God will always help those who have a heart for warfare. We know this was true in David whose heart was that of a warrior and worshipper—this made him a man after God's own heart.

"³⁸All these men of war, who could keep ranks, came to Hebron with a loyal heart, to make David king over all Israel; and all the rest of Israel were of one mind to make David king." 1 Chronicles 12.38

The Lord is a Man of War

"³The LORD is a man of war; the LORD is His name." Exodus 15.3

If we do not face the reality of fighting for what rightfully belongs to us, we will never possess our promises. There is no other way of doing it except to enter the enemy's camp and take it by force! Keeping in mind, our war is not against people but against the devil and his demons.

To exercise lordship means to enforce the laws and will of the Kingdom, on Earth; this is why Scripture refers to us as kings and priests. A priest is one who lifts up sacrifices of prayer and worship to God, but he also exercises dominion over a specific territory and enforces the orders and laws of the Kingdom with the power he received from the Holy Spirit. Are we ready and willing to extend the Kingdom by force? Are we willing to allow God to use us for the changing of stubborn laws—and therefore prohibit abortion, gay marriages, among others? Are we willing to be used by God to establish the Kingdom in our families, businesses, city, and nation? Are we willing to surrender our bodies to the Holy Spirit to extend the Kingdom according to His leading, even when what He asks us to do does not seem to make sense? Your answer cannot be expressed in words; it is a matter of obedience shown through actions. Take heart, the Lord of War is the commander in chief, but are you part of His army?

Let us live as kings and priests of the Kingdom of God, offering sacrifices of praise and establishing His government to the end of the Earth.

BIBLIOGRAPHY

Biblia de Estudio Arco Iris. Reina Valera 1960; Nashville, Tennessee: Broadman & Holman Publishers, 1995.

Biblia Plenitud. Reina Valera 1960; Nashville, Tennessee: Caribe Editorial, 1994.

Biblia Reina Valera 1995. Edición de Estudio; USA: Sociedades Biblicas Unidas, 1998.

Blue Letter Bible. April 12, 2006.
<http://www.blueletterbible.org/index.html>

Brown F., S. Driver, and C. Briggs. *The Brown-Driver-Briggs and English Lexicon.* 9th Ed., Hendrickson, 2005.

Diccionario Español a Inglés, Inglés a Español. Num. 81; Dinamarca, Mexico: Larousse Editorial, 1993.

El Pequeño Larousse Ilustrado, Larousse ed. Barcelona: Editorial Spes, 2002.

James Strong, *The New Strong's Exhaustive Concordance of the Bible.* Nashville, Tennessee: Thomas Nelson, 2001.

Jones, E. Stanley. *The Unshakeable Kingdom and the Unchanging Person.* Washington, USA: Editorial Mc Net Press, 1995.

Lock A. Ward, *Nuevo Diccionario de la Biblia.* Miami, Florida: Unilit Editorial, 1999.

Notes shared by Apostle Alan Vincent on the Kingdom. ©Outpouring Ministries 2005, ©Outpouring Missons International, Inc. 2003. Address: 8308 Fredercksburg Road, San Antonnio, TX 78229 Phone: (210) 614-5650 http://web.iwebcenters.com/outpouring Email: outpouring@outpouringmissions.org

Maldonado, Guillermo. *The Ministry of the Apostle.* 1st ed. FL, USA: ERJ Publicaciones, 2006.

Real Academia Española, *Diccionario de la Lengua Española,* http://www.rae.es

The Amplified Bible. Grand Rapids, Michigan: Zondervan, 1987.

The New American Standard Version. n.p.: Zondervan, n.d.

The Tormont Webster's Illustrated Encyclopedic Dictionary. n.p.: Tormont Publications, 1990.

W.E. Vine, *Diccionario Expositivo de las Palabras del Antiguo Testamento y Nuevo Testamento.* Nashville, Tennessee: Thomas Nelson, 1999. ISBN: 0-89922-495-4.

Webster's New World International Spanish Dictionary English/Spanish. Indianapolis, Indiana: Wiley Publishing, Inc, 2004.

Young, Brad H. *The Parables Jewish Tradition and Christian Interpretation,* 4th ed. Massachusetts, USA: Hendrickson Publisher, LLC, 1998.

www.ingramcontent.com/pod-product-compliance
Lightning Source LLC
Chambersburg PA
CBHW071416090426
42737CB00011B/1483